HEAVEN'S
HEARTBEAT

Personal Reflections on Hearing the Heart of God

A Three-Month Devotional Journey

Micah Smith

iUniverse LLC
Bloomington

HEAVEN'S HEARTBEAT

PERSONAL REFLECTIONS ON HEARING THE HEART OF GOD

iUniverse books may be ordered through booksellers or by contacting:

iUniverse LLC
1663 Liberty Drive
Bloomington, IN 47403
www.iuniverse.com
1-800-Authors (1-800-288-4677)

ISBN: 978-1-4917-0041-9 (sc)
ISBN: 978-1-4917-0040-2 (hc)
ISBN: 978-1-4917-0039-6 (ebk)

Library of Congress Control Number: 2013913172

Printed in the United States of America

iUniverse rev. date: 09/24/2013

To my parents who gave me life.
O.R and Jerri Smith

To my brothers and sisters who made the journey too.

To my wife and best friend, Nancy. (maslnlqf)

To our five children, Ryan, Andrea, Hannah, Jacob
and Ethan, who make me laugh while showing
me what real love looks and sounds like.

And to all who follow,
Listen closely

ACKNOWLEDGEMENTS

This book would not have been possible without the editing skill, unmatched generosity and friendship of Larry Libby and his wife Carol. His gifts have helped and blessed many of the most well known Christian leaders of our time. Yet, he always helps me with a smile and his very best.

Huge thanks to Sharon Seilhymer for her attention to detail and hard work in whipping this baby into shape. God bless you, Sharon! I owe you and Pete another cup of coffee.

I salute the past and present board of directors of Global Gateway Network. Your faith and determination in the harness of plowing the hard ground with me has made it possible. You are friends who hear the father's heart and express it so well. Robert Armstrong, Rodger Carter, Pat Davis, Joanne Erickson, Dicky Hartman, Rick Keyes, Carol Libby, George Midbust, Alan Rither, Greg Smith, Glenn Verheyen.

Thank you will not cover the amazing generosity of Dr. Lorna Schumann and Dr. Karl Tracht and all their associates as they have expressed the heart of God through compassionate medical care in the far-flung places we have traveled. However, I am deeply grateful for them.

The Global Gateway Network support team have all enriched my life and stretched my soul with their volunteer example. In a world that says, "Take, Take, Take." They live, "Give, Give, Give." Linda Minaker, Bill Henshaw and Tom Hall.

To all the pastors and churches, intercessors and friends who hear heaven's heartbeat.

Keep Listening.

FOREWORD

By Larry Libby, an author and editor who
has written a number of books including
Someday Heaven and *Who Made God?*

In the beginning, Micah Smith was only a voice to me.

Carol, my wonderful wife-to-be, served on his pastoral staff in Richland, Washington, and faithfully mailed me cassettes of his weekly messages. There must have been dozens of them… and I listened to every single one.

After losing my first wife to cancer, I'd found myself in a period of prolonged grieving, bordering on depression. Pastor Micah's messages formed one of the strong ropes the Lord used to pull me up out of that dark, hopeless place, and ease me back into sunlit regions once again.

For a long time, I didn't even know what Micah looked like; I just knew the voice. I listened in my SUV on my 25-mile commute to work. I listened in that way-too-empty house of mine, late in the evenings. I listened on my long twilight walks through my neighborhood.

I can't tell you now just what he said that so encouraged my heart, lifted my gaze, gave me courage, and got me moving again. Maybe it was the strong biblical principles. Maybe it was the fresh emphasis on the power and dynamic of the Holy Spirit. Maybe it was the stories about running out on a winding desert road or way up on the ridge of some lonely mountain on one of his many ultra-marathons.

I especially liked the last five minutes of his messages when he would step away from his notes, walk down off the platform, and stand almost in the aisle, urging people to apply the Word of God and take a faith-step in that very moment. (At least, that's how I imagined he did it. I didn't actually see him preach.)

There was comfort in those words, yes, but there was also a firm hand on my back, pushing me into life again. Gradually, I came to believe in adventures yet to be discovered, kingdom tasks I might yet accomplish in the Spirit, and wonderful graces yet to be savored. But I needed to start taking steps of faith to get to those places.

Somehow, it seems fitting that on that beautiful September evening when Carol and I were married, Micah would be the one to tie the knot.

Micah's writing is an extension of his voice—that strong voice, so confident in Christ—that got my feet moving again down the trail of faith. It's engaging, it's compelling, it's biblical, and it lifts up the name of God's Son and my Savior.

I can't think of any better recommendation than that.

INTRODUCTION

Some people may read the title of this book and mistakenly assume that I think I am an expert on what God thinks or might have to say on any given subject. I'm not, believe me when I say, I do not think that for a minute.

If anything, I am a searcher longing to learn to listen to His voice.

No doubt, you could learn more from my mistakes in this story than the things I did right. I'm not a perfect performer. Sometimes I don't want to hear what He has to say. Other times, I am simply distracted by other voices. Or I am doing all the talking and not much listening.

But I have learned a few things about the art of communication with the Lord.

Most importantly, He is patient and persistent with me when I am kicking, squirming and screaming. He is not the out of control, ear piercing, shouter, some would suggest but He does know how to get my attention. Moreover, it is with a firmness, yet gentle touch that is frequently accompanied by such a quiet tone, that I have to be completely still to hear His voice.

Since we are made in God's likeness and image, is it no wonder He wants to spend time with us. Jesus helps us understand God's desire to have personal conversations and open communication with people He loves. That means you! He can give you help that transcends anything available, humanly speaking and He has endless resources to help husbands and wives, parents and children, friends and family, old and young, rich and poor, employer and employee, no matter the language, nation or culture. Jesus became the doorway for you and I to have this kind of relationship with Father God.

My hope is that in some small measure, a few brief glimpses of my story will inspire and spur you to listen closely and keep listening to heaven's heartbeat.

You will find ninety days of personal reflections in this book, yet, you and the Lord can carry on the conversation forever.

Micah Smith, Moyie Springs, Idaho, 2013

PROLOGUE

Bubby was my name as a child. Micah, my older brother, gave it to me. Over the years it changed to Bub and finally to Jack. Micah was a good older brother and has continued to be up to this day. He was by no means perfect, but he provided something that I desperately needed as a child. So, when he asked me to write a foreword for this devotional, I told him that I would read the draft and see if I had anything to say. Privately I was skeptical that I would write a word. As I read the pages he sent, what I found surprised me.

Two ideas jumped off the page at me, the first was uncertainty. Life is uncertain. Micah writes about our Mom being in Israel off and on for several years: *And she (our Mother, Jerri) stayed for most of the next ten years, walking the streets of Jerusalem, praying for God's shalom to rest upon the land and the people.*

The media in the US often portrays Israel as violent and aggressive. I find that ironic, when I listen to the local Washington DC news each morning where rarely a day passes without multiple murders being committed. Or where Channel 4 News stories flash across the screen with ominous regularity from Newtown Connecticut, Fort Hood Texas, Boston, Massachusetts and the many other places in this country where humans wreak havoc and leave a trail of bodies.

What place, what bit of geography, on this Earth provides any certainty for us? Micah included a passage he wrote while in China several years ago. No certainty there. He writes about how this immense uncertainty has created an obsession in our society with the end of the world. *Like a meteor shower falling around us, hordes of apocalyptic messages can make a person wonder what he or she really knows for sure.*

Micah writes of the apathy, separation, and desperation that can overwhelm our minds and destroy our hope for the future. *Even in suffering and separation, you know what I mean, those places where you are on the edge and separated from all perceivable security and it seems that there is no hope and no future…*

The passage that hit me the hardest and the deepest though was about his return to our hometown. With his family, Micah moved back to where we were raised decades after leaving: *It wasn't that I had little, if no good memories growing up, but that some of the bad memories seemed so enormous that there was hardly room for me to see anything else through the window of the past. There was a lot of pain to face on many levels.*

Those few short sentences captured our childhood. Earlier I wrote that Micah was a good older brother and continues to be. I say this because I realized while reading these pages that when we were kids, I always counted on him to protect me and he did. I knew he, along with our Mom, would keep me secure in the uncertain and chaotic world that was our childhood. And that is the other idea that jumped off these pages at me—security.

These pages proclaim over and over the truth that there is no security outside of God and total security in Him—an eternal paradox. It is up to each of us to choose to believe--- to reject the uncertainty of life and rest in the security of God's Grace and Love.

Jack Smith, Ph.D.
Maryland State Department of Education
Chief Academic Officer
2013

A hurricane wind ripped through the mountains
and shattered the rocks before God, but God wasn't
to be found in the wind; after the wind an earthquake,
but God wasn't in the earthquake; and after the
earthquake fire, but God wasn't in the fire; and
after the fire a gentle and quiet whisper.

1 Kings 19:12 (MSG)

—1—

*Jesus told them a story showing that it was necessary
for them to pray consistently and never quit.*
—Luke 18:1-2 (MSG)

Human beings long for a father that believes in them, cheering them on in life. Sadly, many people grow up missing such inspiration and support. The good news is that God wants to be your father and He will never disappoint you or abandon you.

He is cheering for you right now.

Suppose you were able to lay your head on His chest and hear His heartbeat. What do you think you would hear? I believe His heart beats with a rhythm, pulse and cadence that say, "I love you and I want you to hang in there."

He might begin with Luke 18:1. *He doesn't
want you to lose heart and quit.*

Do you see it? Jesus says that prayer is the antidote to losing heart. Allow me to illustrate. In 410 A.D., Rome was brutally crushed and overrun by Alaric I, king of the Visigoths. Imagine this: an angry slave opened the gate of the protected city, the Goths poured in, and for the first time in 800 years, Rome fell to an enemy.

The attack had an overwhelming and disheartening effect upon the believers in Rome. They could not understand why the hub of Christian faith could be ravaged by such evil. Many Christ followers were severely shaken in their faith. Why?

Because they had falsely believed that the strength of their faith was in the invincible stability of Rome.

Many of Jesus' followers today are asking similar questions: "Where is God?" and "Why didn't He stop this?" or "Why does God permit things like this to happen?"

I don't have all the answers but I know God is a good father. As world events continue to darken and people around us lose heart, our call is to be full of His Holy Spirit, move under His touch and share His love and mercy to every person possible. Do not lose heart! Be proactive in your faith.

Look up to your Father in heaven. He is cheering you on to the finish line.

—2—

If you think you are standing strong, be careful not to fall.
—*1 Corinthians 10:12 (NLT)*

The hill was steep, still I was confident I could work my way to the bottom and continue along the creek bed to the north. Snow swirled in sheets, danced in cadence to the wind's call. I moved to my right, taking a couple of quick steps; -- it happened so fast -- I'm still uncertain of the details. My feet didn't just slip, they *leaped* out from under me as if they had a mind of their own, without regard or concern for anything connected above the ankle bone.

Before I could exercise any level of authority over them, my big toes were at eye level. Looking at my feet suspended horizontally before me, I opened my mouth in protest just before I slammed into the ground. I fell hard -- really hard on my back -- with no opportunity to catch myself or soften the landing. In that same instant, I lost every bit of air from my lungs.

My first thought was, *did anyone see me go down?* My second thought was, *Hey, I can't breathe!* Not the slightest wisp of air would move through my lungs. It felt as if the atmosphere around me had collapsed into a vacuum. All I could muster up through my esophagus was a weak "uggggh", as I lay there in the snow on an icy hillside.

Finally, I rolled on my side, managing to lift my head and take a quick survey of the area. Seeing no one who had witnessed my fall, I rolled over on my knees and raised up into a hunched position, half stumbling and half running down the hill and into the trees.

I hadn't planned on falling.

After several more minutes passed, I had gathered myself enough to breathe without pressing my ribs on both sides to help push air in and out. As I moved on, I thought of my flippant confidence as I traversed treacherous ground. A passage from Proverbs scrolled across my mental screen:

First pride, then the crash—
The bigger the ego, the harder the fall.
(Proverbs 16:18)

Storms swept over most of the West -- our area included -- for two weeks it left unusual amounts of snow on the ground. And it continued to snow as I hobbled along the trail back home.

I could have blamed the storm for my fall. After all, it had created the slick, icy conditions. I could have blamed where I live for my fall. From the top of our hill, every direction dropped rapidly at a steep angle. I could have blamed the conditions and the circumstances for my fall. Yet the truth is, the fall was the result of my choice. No one had coerced me to run an icy slope on a stormy day. That bit of wisdom had been mine and mine alone.

The bottom line was simply this: *I didn't think I would fall.* In fact, I couldn't even imagine falling. Not once had it entered my mind! And that realization has led me into some valuable personal reflection.

Experience has a way to coax us into a false sense of security, doesn't it? Experience makes us slick, polished, capable, and vulnerable. What I gained from my painful fall that snowy day was a graphic reminder that *I am not exempt from falling!* Nor is anyone else.

There is another kind of fall, even more dangerous and severe than my abrupt, icy encounter with *terra firma*. It is the fall described in the Bible, both Old and New Testaments, that is the result of a heart neglecting the warning signs of self-sufficiency, self-determination, and self-centeredness. It is a "fall" away from God. The very word *fall* presupposes that one has been in a higher position with Christ. The fall takes one down until they bottom out. For Jonah, it was a great fish. For the prodigal son, it was a pigpen. For Demas, it was the bright lights and siren song of the city (2 Timothy 4:10).

As I trudged up the hill toward home, I made another observation.

Falling and staying down is not God's will for us. Yes, He is the only One who can keep us from falling. Even so, if we *do* fall, He will help us get back up, learn from the experience, and keep going in the energy of the Holy Spirit, which is His grace.

I will not blame circumstances or conditions on any level for my falls; whether those circumstances include stormy economies, icy relationships, or slick temptations.

My feet will learn yet, that "by His power I live and move and exist."

—3—

I said to myself, "Relax and rest.
G<small>OD</small> has showered you with blessings."
—Psalm 116:7 (MSG)

Being a dad and now a grandpa is a gift I cherish. Watching children grow is so fascinating. Stretching beyond infancy, they become toddler live-wires, bursting with energy, full of adventure and curiosity. Their pudgy little fingers, hands and feet can hardly keep up with busy little eyes, looking for the next mystery to unravel and new exploit to conquer.

My wife and I raised five children, so we do have some experience at handling busy, active toddlers. You grab them when they're not looking and hold on tight as they wiggle and worm and challenge your control with every breath.

There have been a few rare and extraordinary moments, however, when these small independent people have relaxed and rested in my arms. It's like heaven and we squeeze and hug and imbibe each other's spirit. When they stop struggling in my arms, we *connect*.

One time while worshipping with a group of leaders, it suddenly dawned on me that there are times when I am so busy, so active, and so full of living energy, bubbling over and full of curiosity and adventure, that Father God knows just how to handle people like me. He grabs me when I'm not looking and holds on tight. Finally, when I realize and understand the gravity of the moment, I relax and we *connect*.

As I rest in His arms, I imbibe His Spirit, I hear His heart and I feel His love. And I am healed and the world is not quite as dark, my problems not so immense and my tears do not sting as much.

Now, stop kicking...

Don't you know he enjoys giving rest to those He loves?
(Psalm 127:2)

—4—

Keep a cool head. Stay alert. The Devil is poised to pounce,
(like a lion) and would like nothing better than to catch you
napping. Keep your guard up. You're not the only ones plunged
into these hard times. It's the same with Christians all over the
world. So keep a firm grip on the faith. The suffering won't
last forever. It won't be long before this generous God who has
great plans for us in Christ—eternal and glorious plans they
are!—will have you put together and on your feet for good.
—1 Peter 5:8-10 (MSG)

*O*k this is going to sound preachy, I agree. Hear me out and I
may make a point to ponder. **People are angry today.** Our
generation has coined new terms for our fuming society.
We joke about someone "going postal" and we read about "road
rage" with a yawn.

It seems like it is only a minute step for men and women
to shift from simple indignation to full-blown fury toward one
another. We see it in parking lots, office cubicles, little league
games and in checkout lines. Ballistic behavior is no respecter
of persons or age. Children in elementary school as well as
high school have mowed down classmates and teachers with
indiscriminate violence. This kind of run-amuck madness kills
marriages, shatters families, ruins ministries, and destroys
minds.

Short fuses stuffed into seething souls. It is like a contagious virus
to be avoided.

The book of Proverbs spells it out: "Don't hang out with angry people; don't keep company with hotheads. Bad temper is contagious—don't get infected" (Proverbs 22:24-25).

The fact is any of us can give a valid list of a dozen reasons to be angry. However, here's the good news. Father God, in His wisdom, designed us with the emotion of anger. Anger is a God-given passion. Martin Luther said he prayed better, preached better and wrote better when angry. Paul says it this way: "Go ahead and be angry. You do well to be angry—but don't use your anger as fuel for revenge. And don't stay angry. Don't go to bed angry. Don't give the Devil that kind of foothold in your life" (Ephesians 4:26-27).

All through the ages, people of great potential have been unraveled by unrighteous anger, missing God's best. It hooked Cain, overcame Moses, swallowed up Jonah, and nearly hung Peter. In Proverbs 29:11 (NLT), Solomon wrote: "Fools vent their anger, but the wise quietly hold it back." And James 1:20 sets the nail, "Human anger does not produce the righteousness God desires."

Your anger can never make things right in God's sight. Our anger left to its own devices leads to death, because it harms others and us. Our anger harnessed and controlled by the Holy Spirit leads to life, because it targets the real soul foe in which there is no light and zero truth.

So, go ahead, be angry. But don't stay angry. Don't use your anger as fuel for revenge. Don't go to bed angry. And by all means of the Spirit, "Don't give the devil that kind of foothold in your life."

—5—

*Each of you should learn to control your own body in
a way that is holy and honorable, not in passionate
lust like the pagans, who do not know God....*
—1 Thessalonians 4:4-6, (NIV)

Apathy is not a word we commonly use these days, at least, not in colloquial English. Usually you hear the word connected to a social or cultural ill in America. For example, we hear about voter apathy, student apathy, and parental apathy and so on. However, there is a kind of apathy, which is equally as deadly as those I have referenced. It is silent and subtle. It is apathy of the soul and spirit. I have some friends who meet once a week and pray together for various needs that may come up. During one such occasion, it was very clear that the Holy Spirit called them to pray and petition heaven for help against apathy. The dictionary defines apathy the following ways:

"Absence of desire or emotion, coolness, unfeeling, impassivity, boredom, indifference, stupor, lethargy, and inertia." I dug a little deeper and discovered that apathy means "a lack of interest in or concern for things that other people find moving or exciting." The Etymology of the word breaks down like this: *Zero emotion.*

Yes, I agree, there are some things that we should not give our passion to (see 1 Thessalonians 4:5). At the same time, however, there is a danger today of believers falling victim to a slumbering indifference, instead of following Jesus with authentic passion.

You see, dear friend, apathy is not only silent and subtle, it will strangle the life of Jesus out of you. No wonder Paul wrote to the church in Rome these strong words: "Another reason for right living is that you know how late it is; time is running out. Wake up, for the coming of our salvation is nearer now than when we first believed" (Romans 13:11, NLT).

Apathy distracts us from keeping the main thing the main thing. It will tighten its noose until the breath of God is cut off. Apathy is our final foe and we need each other in confronting this giant.

More wood on the fire please.

—6—

In his excellent book, *Discipling Nations*, Darrow L. Miller writes, "All people and cultures have a particular model of the universe, or worldview. Their worldview does more to shape their development, their prosperity or poverty, than does their physical environment or other circumstances.... Each worldview creates different cultural stories and produces different values. Ideas produce behaviors and lifestyles that affect people, cultures, nations, and history."

It's true, beliefs influence behavior. I have heard it over and over, like you have, "How could anyone behave in such a way as to hijack a domestic plane load of innocent people and fly the plane into a building with thousands of unsuspecting civilians?"

Ideas do have consequences. Those nineteen men who pirated both United and Delta flights were moved to do so based on their worldview. Let's pause right here, slow down long enough to explore in a personal way what worldview we have adopted. How do you see God? Who is Jesus to you? How do you view other human beings? What do you believe about the Bible? What sources shape your concept of marriage? How about parenting? What ideas have fashioned your view as an employee or employer? What will happen to you when you die?

As you carefully consider questions such as these, please remember this:

13

Reality is not what you say, reality is what you do. And what you do is based upon what you really believe.

I wasn't surprised to find a website called Belief-O-Matic, which states that even if *you* don't know what faith you are, Belief-O-Matic knows. By answering the following questions about your concept of God, the afterlife, human nature, and more, Belief-O-Matic will tell you what religion (if any) you practice, or ought to consider practicing.

Unlike Jesus, Belief-O-Matics has a disclaimer: Warning! Belief-O-Matic assumes no legal liability for the ultimate fate of your soul. Imagine that!

—7—

We are hunted down, but never abandoned by God.
We get knocked down, but we are not destroyed.
—2 Corinthians 4:9 (NLT)

Someone once said that, "those who can, do, those who can't, bully." I know what it feels like to be bullied. Between the ages of seven and ten, I lived near a family of five boys, two of whom made it their hourly mission in life to harass, taunt, tease, chase, and bully me.

As a boy, it felt like hell on earth. They were bigger than me and used every ounce of their size to make my life miserable. Looking back, I'm thankful the day finally dawned when I decided to refuse to live that way any longer. I can still remember the summer evening when these two terrorists caught me behind our house and proceeded to pummel me with kicks, jabs, thumps and punches.

My dad's unexpected presence halted the melee. They instantly jumped off me and I ran over to my dad. As I did, one of them called out, "You just wait, we'll catch you again and we're going to knock your lights out!" Suddenly, something akin to a fearless fire surged in my small soul. I remember I walked a couple of steps in their direction and saying, "No! It stops right now." I then bolted smack into the middle of them and for the first time, gave them a dose of their own punishment. It was a moment of reckoning I shall always remember. I learned a life lesson about the nature of bullies, which by the way, come in all shapes, sizes and age brackets.

What strikes me most vividly about that day is the fact that it was my dad's presence that gave me courage. My surprise attack caught them off guard and it was a good sixty seconds before dad caught up with me and pulled us apart. Those two tormentors lost a victim that day. And I grew a little.

This is my point. Just as there are human bullies, there are also spiritual bullies; demons, principalities, imps of hell who have a single mission with unrelenting zeal; to take you out, pardon the expression, they aim to "Knock your lights out."

One of my friends shared his list of ways we fall victim to the down and "out" schemes of hell. They will drive, discourage and divide us until we burn out, rust out, walk out, play out, sell out, sit out, run out, act out, jump out or check out. Only out is out. No matter what bully, terrorist tactic they use, the result is the same. "You're out!" Bullies are really cowards because they wait to catch you off guard, alone and vulnerable, usually behind closed doors with no witnesses and no evidence (in the traditional sense). Bullies are clever, but you can be clever too.

Here's how to take the bully by the horns, either visible or invisible:

- In Paul's words, "A final word: Be strong with the Lord's mighty power. Put on all of God's armor so that you will be able to stand firm against all strategies and tricks of the Devil. For we are not fighting against people made of flesh and blood, but against the evil rulers and authorities of the unseen world, against those mighty powers of darkness who rule this world, and against wicked spirits in the heavenly realms" (Ephesians 6:10-12, NLT).
- In James' words, "So humble yourselves before God. Resist the Devil, and he will flee from you. Draw close to God, and God will draw close to you" (James 4:7-8, NLT).

- In Peter's words, "Be careful! Watch out for attacks from the Devil, your great enemy. He prowls around like a roaring lion, looking for some victim to devour. Take a firm stand against him, and be strong in your faith" (1 Peter 5:8-9, NLT).
- And in David's words, "My enemies will fall back and perish in your presence" Psalm 9:3 (TLB).

So take it from one who knows from experience, you don't have to tolerate a bully another day! Your Father in Heaven is by your side. Be encouraged and encourage yourself in the Lord. Read 1 Samuel 17:45-50.

A new day has dawned!

—8—

*Now we see things imperfectly as in a poor mirror, but
then we will see everything with perfect clarity. All that I
know now is partial and incomplete, but then I will know
everything completely, just as God knows me now.*
—1 Corinthians 13:12 (NLT)

Nancy, Ethan and I had finished our trek across our great nation; from Washington State to Washington D.C. As we did, the Holy Spirit corrected something out of alignment in my soul. We were tired but not in a bad sort of way, just ready to plant for a season at my brother's house in Maryland.

Yet, as I drove along the dark corridor of MD 301 I knew the Holy Spirit was speaking to me. Neon lights captured my attention as we approached some sort of business on our right. The night was dark and overcast and the neon lights illuminated the area. As I strained to read, what the glowing yellow lights spelled out I had to look twice, "otel and Rest ant".

Of course, some of the lights were out and a few of the letters missing. As a result, some of the message was lost in translation. This could be like "Hotel California" only "Hotel Maryland." Who wants to stay in an "otel and Rest ant" on a dark country Stephen King kind of road? Not me, so we kept on driving.

Yet, I could not escape that Father God was indeed talking to me. It is true, I have been asking Him to give us clarity about our next step, the next decision and the next kingdom chess move.

"So…you want clarity?" He whispered.

"Yes, Lord," I responded. "I want clarity."

"Aren't you willing to walk by faith?" He asked, probing deeper into my soul.

"Well, um, yes, I will walk by faith."

"But what if all the pieces aren't clear? What if you can only see part of the message? Will you still take the step of faith? Will you trust Me if I led you to what looked like a 'Hotel and Restaurant' even if it didn't make sense to you and you didn't have 'clarity'?"

Family and friends alike, I have to tell you that the Lord used this experience to press into my self-sufficiency and desire to have all the answers, to see all the pieces of the puzzle, and have complete clarity in my every day decisions. When it all makes sense *then* I will take the leap of faith and "In God I Trust." However, that is not Father God's way of things. It is not 'His kingdom come or His will be done' way of things.

Jesus told well-intentioned Martha, who loved to be in control, "Didn't I tell you that if you believed, you would see the glory of God?" (John 11:40).

Like you, I was raised with "Seeing is believing" and that is the human reason and rational path. God's path is "Believe and you will see." So, with God's help I have stopped asking for clarity. It will not cross my lips again. He made His point on a dark Maryland highway that I am to walk by faith and not by sight.

This lesson was nailed on the wall of my soul when I read the story of Dr. John Kavanaugh's visit to Mother Teresa's "house for the dying" in Calcutta, India. A brilliant ethicist, Kavanaugh was seeking a clear answer on the direction his life should take. After his arrival, he met Mother Teresa, and she asked him what she could do for him. He asked her to pray for him. Her dark eyes prodded, "What do you want me to pray for?" Kavanaugh's request had brought him halfway around the world: "Pray that I might have clarity."

"No," Mother Teresa responded firmly, "I will not do that."

Surprised by her quick refusal, he asked her why.

"Clarity is the last thing you are clinging to and must let go of," she said.

Kavanaugh looked at her and responded that she always seemed to have clarity about her purpose and mission. Mother Teresa laughed and said, "I have *never* had clarity. What I have always had is trust. So I will pray that you trust God."

If you choose to walk with Christ, you may not find clarity about your dreams, your goals, or your future. You don't get to be in control, either. What you get is a relationship with Christ. What you get is a blessing beyond your wildest imagination. What you get is life abundant and eternal. Just trust. Trust and walk. God's got a great adventure ahead of you and me.

—9—

One day Jesus told his disciples a story to illustrate their need for
constant prayer and to show them that
they must never give up.
—Luke 18:1 (NLT)

In 1943, the world was in a state of chaos and confusion, while global shaking and instability kept people around the world anxious and off balance.

The United States was at war on two fronts and our future was far from certain. At that critical moment in history, however, a diverse community of men and women had secretly come together around a common cause, pouring their energies into a common purpose.

In just two years' time, they literally changed the course of human history. Not forty-five miles from where I grew up, a monument stands to their hard work and sacrifice.

This highly secret endeavor became known as the Manhattan Project, and you would have to delve deeply into history to find a better example of intense cooperation and profound productivity in such a very short time frame. Under the direction of U. S. Army General Leslie Groves, military and civilian sectors worked side by side. Scientists, engineers, construction workers, and managers joined their experience, skills, and dedication to build the world's very first large-scale plutonium producing nuclear reactor.

From the day this community of visionaries broke ground for the project, it was roughly thirteen months later, on September 26, 1944, when the now historic 100-B reactor went critical. It was an unparalleled feat of proactive teamwork and radical commitment.

Can you imagine how thousands of people from all over the United State -- with no precedents or patterns from which to build -- created something so revolutionary in so little time? I took my entire family on the sixtieth anniversary tour of the 100-B reactor, which my dad helped build in 1943-44.

Whatever your opinion of nuclear power might be in these unstable days, allow me to make this comparison: A community of Christ-following men and women who will pray and serve together with passion and persistence can have a greater impact on our time than the unleashing of the atom, back in the 1940s.

Talk about critical mass. Can you envision a spiritual chain reaction? Can you see, with eyes of faith, kingdom fission and fusion rippling across the world?

In the first eight verses of Luke 18, a persistent widow demonstrates the quality that enables any community of pioneers to stick together and break new ground. The woman in this story kept coming back again and again and again and again. And eventually, she triumphed.

The woman shows us how to stick with it. Only the most persistent, hardheaded, bothersome, stubborn, unrelenting, and enduring make a meaningful difference. People like this exhibit unfailing stamina and fortitude in the face of seemingly insurmountable opposition and doubt.

On the other hand, it isn't just human persistence alone, it is persistence *in prayer*, linked to the greatest Source of power in the universe that will lead to transformation and change on this troubled planet we call home.

Crack open your Bible and read about the Messiah Project in the book of Acts. The team is still coming together ... and there's room for you.

—10—

There is a time for everything...
a time to cry and a time to laugh.
—Ecclesiastes 3:1-4 (NLT)

Joshua led Israel into God's promises, which were filled with both blessings and battles. People tend to think in either/or terms about most things. We are naturally conditioned to think in either/or terms of winners/losers, black/white, right/wrong, success/failure and good/bad, for example. But either/or thinking is not always accurate or applicable to every circumstance or situation. Sometimes it is "both."

Let me explain. Perhaps you heard these words or even thought them recently, "We are living in perilous times." The word perilous as I would define it in my own words means "delusional insanity." Greater, larger and more illuminating than our times of delusional insanity is the presence of Christ in us.

We do live in tough times. There are immense challenges and obstacles in front of us. Yet, we have the presence of One who is "greater than he that is in the world."

It is both. The psalmist got it right in 34:19: "Many evils confront the righteous, but the Lord delivers him out of them all." (AMP) Again, it is both evil confrontations and the Lord's deliverance.

Optimists are not always right. Neither are pessimists. Life is about both the positives and the negatives.

I embrace the truth of both and believe it leads to authentic fulfillment in Christ. Why? Because if our thinking slips into neutral gear of either/or, we may simply face "our present troubles" with a fatalistic shrug and a sigh, while not recognizing Jesus' delivering presence.

It's not always "either/or." Sometimes it's "both."

—11—

*It is better to trust the L*ORD *than to put confidence in people.*
—Psalm 118:8 (NLT)

I can't quote the prophecy word for word, but the message was clear:

"Some of you have a deficient expectation, and if you continue on this course you will have a collision with disappointment. You have become comfortable and you must reexamine your priorities."

The implication was unarguable. Father God was gently, yet firmly, correcting a common but misguided mindset. It is not uncommon to come across people who verbalize such thinking as,

- When I marry this person, all my troubles will be solved.
- If I can get to know so and so… then I can achieve….
- This man or this woman or this group will fulfill my vision for ministry.
- This church will heal my emotionally broken family.
- My best friend will never let me down. Please indulge me… once more.
- If this man (or woman) becomes president, smooth sailing ahead.

On and on it goes. Moreover, it is not true!

The prophetic word provided me with principle for life. Please memorize it. Write it down and never forget it: *"Deficient expectations and disappointment travel together."* Every pre-marriage class should hear those words. Every business partnership should take notice. Every couple thinking that having a baby will heal their marriage had better rethink that decision. Every church looking to a pastor as the solution to their dreams had better sit down and invest some time in praying through their priorities.

The fact is, when you expect another human -- any human -- to be "the answer," you have at that moment set yourself up for disappointment. Father God did not wire us to be the answer for other human beings' expectations. Not even so-called *powerful people.* In fact, Scripture says as much: "Don't put your confidence in powerful people; there is no help for you there" (Psalm 146:3, NLT).

God isn't kidding here. He goes on to say, "This is what the LORD says: 'Cursed are those who put their trust in mere humans and turn their hearts away from the LORD. They are like stunted shrubs in the desert, with no hope for the future. They will live in the barren wilderness, on the salty flats where no one lives. But blessed are those who trust in the LORD and have made the Lord their hope and confidence. They are like trees planted along a riverbank, with roots that reach deep into the water. Such trees are not bothered by the heat or worried by long months of drought. Their leaves stay green, and they go right on producing delicious fruit'" (Jeremiah 17:5-8, NLT).

Did you notice the contrast of curse and blessing, barrenness and fruitfulness, rootless and stable, peace and anxiety? The one and only difference in these two kinds of people is where they place trust and expectation.

Have you ever had someone say to you, "I stuck my neck out for you!"? Usually when they crash in on you with words like these, it's because they really did stick their neck out, *and now they are headless and disappointed.*

The next time you are tempted to stick your neck out, make sure you are doing it for the right reason and in the right direction. *Up!* Only Jesus can satisfy. Well... what did you expect? As it says in Scripture: "I will satisfy my people with my bounty. I, the Lord, have spoken!" (Jeremiah 31:14, NLT)

If you don't believe this is serious... buckle up.

—12—

Where there is no vision, the people perish.
—Proverbs 29:18 (KJV)

A couple of days before my dad died, right before he slipped away into God's presence, the clarity in his eyes faded. The crisp, sharp, fiery green was gone. Now, opaque and cloudy, like an overcast sky, my dad was blind.

What I learned from those last heart-rending moments is that his vital organs were shutting down and now, after eighty years of doing the business called life, the lights were going out, all the rooms were being emptied and his body was dying.

Did you know that same sequence is true of a believer and even a local church? A Christian or a church without vision is in the final throes of death.

One wise guy, prompted by the Holy Spirit wrote as much in Proverbs 29:18. Here are a few different renderings of that verse for you to chew on... or should I say, "see."

Where there is no vision, the people perish. (KJV)
When people do not accept divine guidance, they run wild.
But whoever obeys the law is happy. (NLT)
If people can't see what God is doing,
they stumble all over themselves;
But when they attend to what he reveals,
they are most blessed. (MESSAGE)

Certainly, Paul was familiar with this Proverb. As he traveled around casting the seed of Jesus' message to the Gentile nations, I wonder if he became somewhat of a moonlighting optometrist?

His track record reveals that he had the least amount of spiritual optometry in a city called Ephesus, which happened to have the church that prayed often and saw much. It seems Ephesus believers had healthy, spiritual eyesight.

The kingdom of God was at hand but it was also in the eyes of these people. Paul had a blast in the city of Ephesus. He really did. You can read about his exciting activity in Acts chapter 19. There is little doubt that Ephesus stands out among other New Testament church models for true, God-sent restoration.

Notice Paul's opening words in Ephesians 1:17-19: "I ask the God of glory to make you intelligent and discerning in knowing Him personally, your eyes focused and clear, so that you can see exactly what it is He is calling you to do; grasp the immensity of this glorious way of life He has for Christians. Oh, the utter extravagance of His work in us who trust Him... endless energy and boundless strength!"

Did you get that? Paul prays for these already loving, praying people to see with eyes that are focused and clear; which releases endless energy and boundless strength to live out God's purposes in your city, state, nation and world.

By the way, have you noticed what word is left if you take away the first "E" from the word "eyes"? Yes is the response God is looking for, as we live our lives for Him. "Yes" will keep your eyes clear.

I can see that.

—13—

By faith these people overthrew kingdoms, ruled with justice, and received what God had promised them. They shut the mouths of lions, quenched the flames of fire, and escaped death by the edge of the sword. Their weakness was turned to strength. They became strong in battle and put whole armies to flight. Women received their loved ones back again from death. But others were tortured....
—Hebrews 11:32-40 (NLT)

Faith in action inspires people. Who wouldn't want to see a guy walk on water, walk through fire or produce water from a rock? On the other hand, lest I be less than accurate, faith can be intimidating. Notice that it is the same vein of faith that empowers kingdom people to be "tortured."

I can see it now....

COME TO THE FAITH CRUSADE JUNE 22-28, AND LEARN
HOW TO BE CUT IN TWO, RIPPED APART, AND BEATEN TO A PULP!

Has it ever occurred to you that the same faith that empowers you to *enlarge* is the same faith that empowers you to *endure*? Enlarging never happens without enduring and subduing has an element of the scary in it. And it is this unique mix of faith in action, which is so contagious.

So are discontent, melancholy and doubt. Just ask Caleb and Joshua. Someone said that a "ship in the harbor is safe but that is not what ships are made for." How true. Even more sobering is the fact that men and women of the kingdom are safe in their recliner, office and hot tub. But that is not what men and women of the kingdom were made for, is it? I think not.

We can read the record and hear the stories of kingdom people who got out of the boat, jumped into a den of lions, faced giants, out ran chariots and used the jawbone of an ass to take out an army of a thousand and it contagiously inspires us.

What we don't know is how many stories were short-circuited, diffused and not realized because people of the kingdom remained in the safe harbor of convenience and unbelief, resting in the recliner of the familiar, thus avoiding the intimidating side of faith?

Wait just a moment! They also miss the inspiring, enlarging side of faith. My observations have nothing to do with perceived accusations toward others, instead it is the day in and day out temptations I face in the corridors of my own soul. I don't want to finish life saying, "What might have been?"

Do you?

—14—

Later, a great many people from the Gerasene countryside got together and asked Jesus to leave — too much change, too fast, and they were scared. So Jesus got back in the boat and set off.
—Luke 8:37 (MSG)

Some wisecrack once said that the "only constant in life is change." Before I ride over the philosophical waterfall and disappear in the froth and foam hoping to bob up on the surface down river, let's imagine that the wise guy is accurate in his observation. Change is scary and something akin to riding a canoe over a waterfall; it's also dangerous.

Dr. Luke describes with graphic preciseness how human nature often responds to change as he re-tells the story of Jesus' wonderful miracle on the east shore of the lake called Galilee. You remember, don't you? Jesus encounters a man fully controlled by a mob of tormenting demons that have completely dehumanized him. His family could do nothing. His Church could do nothing. His community could do nothing. The only constant in his life was wretchedness; until he met Jesus.

One would think that his family, church and community would hail Jesus with celebrations of joy and festive relief. But not so, as Luke points out; they asked Jesus to leave. Why? "Too much change, too fast and they were scared." There it is ... the bottom line in understanding people's reticence to change. They were scared. The Greek word is "phobos," and it is connected to another word you will recognize, "megas."

The rapid change apparently sent them in a tailspin of mega-fear, big panic, huge-terror and immense-dread. Get the picture? It really is kind of like going over a waterfall, complete with sweaty palms, high blood pressure and dilated pupils.

Change does that to some people more than others, it's true. However, change does not have to be such a terrifying experience. We all experience change. We cannot avoid change. It would be nice if we could set our life up as one constant, but the truth is, life is not static.

Change is life. Stagnation is death. If you don't change, you die. It's that simple and that scary. The cells in your body are constantly being replaced -- you're always in flux. The universe is expanding. Change is here to stay. The people of the Gerasene countryside probably were not aware of Jesus' pronouncement as recorded by Dr. Luke in Luke 12:50: "I've come to change everything, turn everything right-side up."

My familial journey has brought about all of the elements and dimensions of being excited and scared because of change. Nonetheless, when I read Jesus' words in Luke 12, I am reminded once again, we don't have to fear waterfalls.

—15—

I don't know about you, but I'm running hard for the finish line.
I'm giving it everything I've got. No sloppy living for me! I'm staying
alert and in top condition. I'm not going to get caught napping,
telling everyone else all about it and then missing out myself.
—1 Corinthians 9:26-27 (MSG)

Please understand that I understand that most people think I am weird or just running "from" something, when they hear that my hobby is trail running in the mountains. I've seen them roll their eyes and twist their lips into the shape of cauliflower as they quickly change the subject or merely walk away. And I agree, ultra trail-runners are a peculiar sliver of humanity. Before you hit that delete button, hear me out and perhaps you will capture a brief glimpse into what drives this passion. For me, trail running is an incubator, a microcosm of life, if you will. The dirt, the trees, the waterfalls and the steep, technical terrain teach me about focus, determination and feelings. Yes, feeling, because during a long endurance trail run your emotions can change as rapidly as the elevation or the weather.

I've learned to avoid some of life's pitfalls from the ruts and roots and rocks that I must navigate on the trails. I've run into mountain lions, moose and rattle snakes. I have felt the euphoria of a light rain cascading down my face in old growth timber and the pure unadulterated joy of fragrant fields of wild flowers, strewn across a high mountain meadow.

I also know what it means to be completely consumed with one four-letter word: QUIT. I have fallen, tripped by some unseen or unobserved peril, rising up at the right time in the wrong place, only to get up bloodied and hurting, knowing I must continue down the trail. And I have never yet, one time regretted crossing the finish line; the satisfaction is unmatched.

Here are some of my favorite quotes from a handful of famous people.

- "Relentless Forward Motion." (Covey)
- "When was the last time you did something for the first time?" (Kobi Yamada)
- "Obstacles are what you see when you take your eyes off of the goal." (Escobar)
- "Do or do not, there is no try." (Yoda)
- "Life is not a journey to the grave with the intention of arriving safely in a pretty and well preserved body, but rather to skid in broadside, thoroughly used up, totally worn out, and loudly proclaiming, "WOW! What a ride!" (Unknown)
- "The woods are lovely, dark and deep, but I have promises to keep, and miles to go before I sleep, and miles to go before I sleep." (Robert Frost)
- And finally, "Fear the chair."

I don't know who coined that last phrase, "fear the chair," but I know what it means. Ultra runners are conscious of the fact that after running for several hours the temptation to sit down in a chair at one of the aid stations is enormous. And if you give in to the temptation, your body stiffens and locks up like a bank vault and your progress to the finish line is seriously hampered.

Look at it through this lens. Some people start the race of life, running well and strong over the exciting landscape of college, career and marriage.

Life is an adventure but it's also dangerous. The first scary surprise is navigated and then the first fall comes. Ok, get up and keep moving. Then another fall, another scare, another trip and fall, another detour and life has a way of losing its zest. The flowers no longer hold their fragrant, colorful appeal. The mountains only make us tired and before we realize what is happening, we reach mid-life, dragging into the next aid station we find a chair and sit down and quit the race of life and give up the dream.

The only problem with this decision is you lose your resilience and elasticity. You freeze up and life keeps going. Where once you ran strong at the start, now you are unable to run at all.

Interestingly enough, Jesus never asked people how they started the race. He did however, ask them how they would finish. It is the finish line of life that matters most. That is why ultra endurance trail runners "fear the chair."

Keep running!

—16—

Fight the good fight for what we believe.
—*1 Timothy 6:12 (NLT)*

The driveway to our house and small farm appeared to be a gauntlet of raw nerves and apprehension; at least to a seventh grade boy it did. At the end of that driveway was my dad, and I had just been expelled from school for three days.

Dad used language that I didn't always understand, and as I grew, I came to learn that some of his language was not to be repeated in mixed company, as well as other expressions, born from his deep southern roots, that I've thought about for years.

"Son," he would tell me, "You have to face the music." What music? I strained my ears, but I never could hear music in those moments.

My feet felt like two lead weights as dust swirled around my shoes dragging one foot in front of the other. I found him back by the barn and the first thing he asked me was what I feared most, "Why are you home from school early?" The words stuck in my parched throat, finally managing to choke them out, "I was expelled from school."

He didn't look up from what he was doing as he asked, "What for?" I knew I had to tell him. There was no way out of it. I was backed into a corner and now the moment of reckoning was upon me.

"Fighting," I responded.

"Did you start the fight?" he asked.

41

"No. Well... I don't think I did."

The truth was I was as much to blame as the boy I got into a fight with. Since that day, I've learned a great deal about fighting and some of the lessons were hard and difficult to learn. Fighting in and of itself is not necessarily a bad thing. Sometimes there are righteous reasons to fight; to protect the innocent, our families and our very lives can be proper and right motivation to engage in conflict.

Other times and observed only by Father God, wrong motives drive conflict and fighting ensues between husbands and wives, parents and children, coworkers, neighbors and church members. Even nations have engaged in hostilities over wrong motives.

At the end of the driveway, Father God waits to ask us what is driving the battle. James describes what it means to face the music,

"You want what you don't have, so you scheme and kill to get it. You are jealous of what others have, but you can't get it, so you fight and wage war to take it away from them. Yet you don't have what you want because you don't ask God for it. And even when you ask, you don't get it because your motives are all wrong" (James 4:2-3, NLT).

Post script. The boy I got into a fight with in seventh grade died when he was fifty years old. Our local newspaper reported that he had been dead for two weeks before deputies found him. His neighbors said few people came by his house, a yellow country house with no air conditioning surrounded by tall grass and aging trucks. "When we were out here working he would talk to us. I don't think he had good friends. He was sick and appeared despondent and disheartened."

The neighbors went on to say in the article, "Nobody was there to help him."

I wish I had known, I would have faced the music with him once again.

—17—

But since you excel in everything—in faith, in speech, in knowledge,
in complete earnestness and in the love we have kindled in you—
see that you also excel in this grace of giving.
—2 Corinthians 8:7, (NLT)

*H*ave *you ever noticed how children give?* There is no doubt that they often learn one word all by themselves, "Mine." Yet, when they decide to share it is not only fun to watch but also an adventure to explore.

I can remember so clearly the generosity of my kiddos when they were small. Without hesitation, any one of them would lift up their cool, refreshing bottle of root beer, orange crush or cream soda and offer me a drink. I would raise the bottle up, gaze into the sweet liquid, see all of those back washed, new life forms and hand the bottle back. Indeed, with child-like grace, they wanted to share with me. I love that! As they grew, I grew too. There finally came the time when I would take the bottle, close my eyes and drink. What a fantastic bonding experience.

Does it surprise you that Paul includes giving as one of the key Christian virtues, right there alongside faith, speech, knowledge, and love? It shouldn't. The Bible speaks clearly regarding giving. We are to give to God "our best," "the first fruits of our labor," "generously," and "with great joyfulness."

As the Holy Spirit changes our lives, He changes the way we look at money. My children never got trapped in the "He's my daddy, I have to give him a drink" way of thinking. They really wanted to share with me. Believe me when I say, that influenced my response to their offer. Neither should we get caught in the trap of "forced giving," where giving becomes a slavish duty.

Smile at your Father in heaven and share what He has given you. In doing so, you will help change the world.

—18—

My beloved friends, let us continue to love each other since love comes
from God. Everyone who loves is born of God and experiences a
relationship with God. The person who refuses to love doesn't know the
first thing about God, because God is love—so you can't know him if
you don't love. This is how God showed his love for us: God sent his
only Son into the world so we might live through him. This is the kind
of love we are talking about—not that we once upon a time loved
God, but that he loved us and sent his Son as a sacrifice to clear away
our sins and the damage they've done to our relationship with God.
—1 John 4:7-10 (MSG)

The questions rolled around my brain like a marble on a roulette wheel. *How do I measure my ability to love?* I'm not talking about a love defined by the culture here, rather a love transformed by Christ.

I have stood before adults and children, holding my arms outstretched symbolizing the cross, while saying, "Jesus loves you this much... and then He died." *Is that it, then? Is the distance between my outstretched arms the true measurement of love?* When my children were small, I would stretch my arms apart in similar fashion while looking into their bright eyes and tell them, "Daddy loves you this much!"

Is that really how much I love?

Without sinking into a mishmash of personal navel-gazing, this is part of my journey. It is sad to think that as a believer and follower of Jesus for many years, I am wondering about my spiritual love quotient. Nevertheless, I am.... which has given me even more motivation to probe this tender spot.

In Matthew 24:12-13, Jesus prophetically saw and stated that a signpost of the end of time would be a cold dip in people's ability to *give and receive* authentic love. Resting on the Mount of Olives with His disciples, looking out over Jerusalem, Jesus fixed His gaze upon the city, the people, and the world that He loved. Then it says He wept.

How do I know He loved them? By what He gave... His very life. Could that be the measure of love? Not so much what I *do*, but rather by what I am willing to give up? Does a yardstick or the distance between outstretched arms measure love?

At the end of life what is more important than love? The kind of love that never gives up... cares more for others than for self... doesn't force itself on others... isn't always "me first"... doesn't fly off the handle... doesn't keep score of the sins of others... doesn't revel when others grovel... takes pleasure in the truth... trusts God always... always looks for the best... never looks back... but keeps going to the end.

—19—

*But the angel assured her, "Mary, you have nothing to fear.
God has a surprise for you."*
—Luke 1:30 (MSG)

You are aware that not all surprises are a sure prize, aren't you? For example, picture me running down a mountain trail with panoramic views, extraordinary blue sky, sunshine and 70 degrees when suddenly I am ferociously attacked from behind. My mind instantly goes into over drive, racing wildly, as I am assaulted by an unknown foe. The speed and velocity with which I am hit delays any tactical response. I am overwhelmed with paralysis and the confusion grabs time and motion by the throat until everything around me slows down to the speed of molasses on a cold November day.

In the ten seconds required for all of this to happen, I re-take control of my vocal chords and force an unwilling scream from the depths of my being into the clear mountain air. It is so violent that my adversary drops to the ground beside me. I turn quickly to face this terrorist and find myself toe to toe with a two-pound and wildly upset male grouse. Now, I have faced down a mountain lion and a mother moose with a calf. Trees have narrowly missed me as they have fallen along the trail as I ran. Yet, up to this point, I have never met a more terrible, no good and very rotten, fowl character as this one in the woods. I truly understate my point when I say I was surprised!

The word surprise has a rich history going back to the 15th century. The noun as we know it was given birth from the French word *surprendre*, which means "to take over." And it has grown to include the idea of "something exceptionally desirable." I like that!

As with many places in the West, Germany has had a flood of refugees and immigrants streaming across its borders. On one of my frequent visits to Germany, I was deeply impressed by the grace of God I saw in the lives of some very unexpected people. A man from Azerbaijan, with joy and peace in his eyes, spoke of loving Jesus, "the Most High God." A widow in Afghanistan shared how Jesus appeared to her in visions to encourage and comfort her. Arriving in Germany, she told me, she could not read or write the language. She had five children and felt very sad at times. Yet, in those moments of deepest sorrow, Jesus had brought her incredible comfort.

One small group I met with included a brand new believer from China, deeply hungry for the Bible. He was bringing a Chinese girl to the group meetings, who I imagine was very close to being surprised by God.

I'm overtaken with the message, God sent Mary, the mother of Jesus, *"I have a surprise for you, dear one."* Do you know what? That is His message to you today. Let Him surprise you. Allow Him to take over whatever is hurting or haunting you. In its place Jesus will bring forth something exceptionally desirable and I am pretty sure it won't be a wild-eyed grouse attacking you from behind as you run through the woods.

Grouse fettuccine, Hmmmm...

—20—

*Don't love the world's ways. Don't love the world's goods. Love of
the world squeezes out love for the Father. Practically everything
that goes on in the world—wanting your own way, wanting
everything for yourself, wanting to appear important—has
nothing to do with the Father. It just isolates you from him. The
world and all its wanting, wanting, wanting is on the way
out—but whoever does what God wants is set for eternity.*
—1 John 2:15-17 (MSG)

Fairy tales begin with the words "Once upon a time..." The story I am about to share is true. In 1772, Franz Joseph Haydn wrote his piece called the *Farewell Symphony for Prince Nikolaus Esterhazy of Austria.* As typical for symphonies, Haydn wrote Farewell in four movements. He designed the piece for two oboes, a bassoon, two horns and violins divided into two violas, cellos and double basses.

He wrote the pathos-filled symphony because his musicians were frustrated and wanted to leave the country palace of the prince and return to their families. As the Prince sat listening to the new symphony he must have been stunned when the first oboe closed the music on his stand, blew out his candle and tiptoed from the stage. The second horn followed. One by one, the other wind instruments were silenced as the musicians got up, blew out their candles and left the orchestra. At last, only the conductor and two muted violins were left. With each departing musician, the light of another candle was extinguished and the room dimmed a darker shade. As the candlepower diminished, the symphony lost another unique sound of a silenced instrument until the music faded into a palpable emptiness.

In some ways, this is a haunting story because it could describe the story of my generation. Without being overly bleak or generalizing the subject, I hardly think any American could truthfully argue against the fact that for the past fifty years one cultural candle at a time has been extinguished. Nor could one deny that the beauty of God's lyrics are not so much as mentioned in America's top 40 any longer.

In many instances, the syncretism adopted by American Christians, has dimmed their divine light by way of an easy believe-ism; a kind of intellectual gospel of convenience. Really, nothing more than a deep love affair with the world.

With creative variety, Jesus tells His followers repeatedly in the Gospels that we are God colors, God flavoring and God lyrics on the public stage.

Yes, some of the God-conducted instruments have been silenced, but there are yet, tens of thousands of spiritual musicians playing God's lyrics to the Holy Spirit's beat and the Prince is watching.

—21—

"Do you want to stand out? Then step down. Be a servant…
if you're content to simply be yourself, your life will count for plenty."
—Matthew 23:11-12 (MSG)

It is not possible for me to grasp how quickly the past twenty-five years have slipped by; on second thought that is not an accurate observation. Some of them did not merely slip silently into the night of my history; many of them were loud, impetuous, and in-my-face years.

When Nancy and I were appointed to our first pastorate at age twenty-five, I felt like a loose 220-volt wire with no connection. In other words, I had no idea if I was doing the right things at the right times and places for the right reasons. There were often undercurrent feelings of "I must be missing something and it's 'out there' somewhere."

It was about my thirtieth birthday when I finally got it. The search for significance is not "out there" somewhere. *I discovered it really is an "inside" job.* Jesus Himself said, "If you're content to simply be yourself, your life will count for plenty."

As I ponder that truth, I think of Jesus' Palm Sunday steed. Luke 19 and Matthew 21 give us a clear picture of Jesus entering Jerusalem, not in a warrior's chariot, certainly not mounted on a white stallion, but riding a donkey. This small clip-clopping charger would barely lift Jesus above the standing press of the crowd. Nevertheless, He submitted to God's wonderful and infallible plans. He carried the Messiah *and he never pretended to be a horse.* He simply did what he was created to do: use his strong back and sure feet to bear God's gift to the world. Sounds like a local church to me.

No wonder the donkey is the only animal in the Bible that talks.

Hee-haw!

—22—

And He did it, rescued us from certain doom. And He'll do
it again, rescuing us as many times as we need rescuing.
—2 Corinthians 1:10 (MSG)

One October, I found myself in a hellish predicament with a burden that was almost too great to carry. It all started when two of my sons, Ryan and Jacob, joined me on a trip to the wild Hell's Canyon area in northeastern Oregon.

My first mistake was telling myself a lie. This is a painful process and one that should not be repeated under any circumstances. On the other hand, the problem is that when you are deceived you don't know it. And self-deception always starts by telling yourself a big fat lie and then in rapid-fire succession, you move without forethought to "believe it" and act on it before anyone has the time to try and talk some sense into your head.

We told ourselves that we were going into some of the most remote and beautiful country in the West for a pleasant deer hunting trip, when in reality we were about to be throttled by the vertical and malicious mountains around the Snake River's infamous Hell's Canyon.

As I sat perched on a narrow ribbon of basalt rock six miles into the growing truth of what I had done I thought of two things: One, the words of the great and late Louis L'Amour who said, "mountains and women have this in common, for they are the two places where both beauty and terror ride together." And secondly, that this was the closest thing to dumb I had done in a long time. Sometimes I wonder, will I ever learn?

It was then that I laughed at myself and asked God to help me. He did and I made it to the top of the mountain with my burden intact at the edge of Hell's Canyon.

You know, it is when we feel like we've been deceived, over burdened and this predicament is like hell, that Jesus steps in to help us shoulder the load. Yet, we have to be willing in our dirty and disheveled shape, to ask for His help, laugh at ourselves in the process and keep climbing because at the end of the day the only thing that makes us fully human is our willingness to admit our mistakes, ask for help and laugh through it all.

The payoff comes at the top because the view is worth it. When I stood on top of that mountain at sunset, I knew that only God could turn curses into blessings. The good news is that Jesus doesn't ask you where you've been or why you started this climb, we call life. What He wants to know is how you finish. Can you laugh at your foibles and failings? Especially in difficult times, can you find the humor in the situation you're in?

Old Uncle Enoch Hull, a mountain man from the south whose body was bent and distorted with arthritis, sat in church one Sunday morning. All the older members of the congregation except Uncle Enoch arose and gave testimony to their religious experiences. Uncle Enoch kept his seat. Thereupon the moderator said, "Brother Enoch, suppose you tell us what the Lord has done for you."

Uncle Enoch arose with his bent and distorted body, and said, "Brother, He has mighty blessed me! But those mountains, those mountains nigh ruint me."

What I learned again on the mountain near hell is that Jesus' rescue operation always makes me smile in the midst of adversity. And sometimes.... sometimes, I laugh out loud.

—23—

Then Hezekiah said to Isaiah, "This message you have given me from the LORD is good." But the king was thinking, "At least there will be peace and security during my lifetime."
—*Isaiah 39:8 (NLT)*

Somehow, I think it is bred into us, I really do. The word *coward* revolts most Americans. I cannot think of anyone I know who would relish being called a coward. There is only one step down from cowardice and that is being a traitor. The tag of coward is one of the most despised of all human qualities. We will do almost anything to avoid being called a coward.

I remember when I was in grade school and a kid would dare someone in our crowd to do something we all knew was dumb but some of us would do it anyway just to avoid the taboo title of *Chicken*. We don't want to be a chicken and we certainly do not want to be called a chicken, do we? No, we would rather face something that scares the living daylights out of us than receive that brand.

We love courageous people. We despise the cowardly. In every movie, the bad guys are usually spineless cowards and people hate them for it. In our families, fathers always want their wives and children to see them as being courageous because that's the kind of material heroes are made of.

Usually, when we think of courage, we think of death defying acts, great and heroic sacrifices. We think of firemen going into burning buildings and bringing out children. We think of soldiers falling on a grenade to save their buddies. We think of policemen in the line of fire. We think of astronauts and Holocaust survivors. We picture Congressional Medal of Honor winners.

Americans love heroes and that is a great thing about us. More often than not, enormous amounts of courage are required just to face the ordinary challenges of everyday life and do the right thing.

Every day we make choices. We get to choose what path we walk, courageous or cowardly. There should be no illusions about the fact that courage is an essential ingredient if we are going to make a difference in our world. Changed people change the world. You can't change the world by imitating it, by impressing it, by waving peace placards for it, or blending in with it.

Jesus said in John 16:33 (NLT), *"Here on earth you will have many trials and sorrows...."*

Notice it's not an option. It's going to happen so don't be surprised. He went on to say, *"But take heart, because I have overcome the world."*

—24—

And he called his ten servants, and delivered them ten pounds,
and said unto them, Occupy till I come.
—Luke 19:13 (KJV)

Western culture is obsessed with time. Have you ever counted all the clocks you see in just one day? Take an easy test to check out my observation. How many timepieces do you have in your house? You would think that with all of our clocks, calendars, watches, day timers, daily planners and smart phones, our lives would be simpler and less complicated, however it simply isn't true, is it?

Could it be that in spite of the many ways we measure time that we are still missing the point? Are we measuring time correctly? What if we were so focused on measuring years, months, days, hours, minutes, seconds and even nano-seconds that we missed the *epochs* of God, those divine periods of opportunity on God's overarching time-line?

Jesus made an interesting point using time as His backdrop. His assembled servants are given a sum of money and told that during the period of time of His absence they were to (Old English) occupy, until He returned.

What a fascinating choice of words. Occupy means to "take possession of," or "to seize." The Greek word is "prag-mat-yoo'-om-ahee." Those of us who speak English derive our word "Pragmatic" or "Practical" from this word. In essence, Jesus was saying use your resources in practical ways to fulfill a spiritual mandate. I like how Message says it, "But first he called ten servants together, gave them each a sum of money, and instructed them, "Operate with this until I return." (Luke 19:13)

Here's the point. This is the best time in history for kingdom people to maximize their resources for taking territory for the kingdom. No, I am not referring to real estate or geography, at least not in a physical sense.

However, I think there is an essential kingdom principle that we dare not miss. Through the years, I have listened to a good number of well-meaning believers, people who love God with all of their hearts who have intentionally taken a passive posture toward life. Somehow, they have allowed a mindset to subtly slip in and strip them of any proactive responsibility. It is as though the great commission and the great commandment are fulfilled and accomplished in a mystical, ethereal, almost metaphysical way. This out of kilter, abstract approach has led many a loved one of God down the pathway of regret. By the time they finally get the point, the time for them to act and move in practical ways has long sense passed them by.

Am I suggesting that we humans carry the sole responsibility of advancing the kingdom apart from God? Of course not... we need the Holy Spirit's help. After all, He is God. He counsels, guides, corrects, grants wisdom and discernment to "occupy and operate" until Jesus returns.

James may have said it best, "Dear friends, do you think you'll get anywhere in this if you learn all the right words but never do anything? Does merely talking about faith indicate that a person really has it? Isn't it obvious that God-talk without God-acts are outrageous nonsense? You can no more show me your works apart from your faith than I can show you my faith apart from my works. "Faith and works, works and faith, fit together hand in glove." James 2:14, 17-18 (MSG).

What's the bottom line? Have faith in God, pray without ceasing and then use your mind, your skills, your gifts, your passion, your personality, your position in life, your hands, your voice, your feet, your resources and your influence to advance the kingdom through your simple, practical, courageous deeds. That's what it means to occupy.

Talk about making the most of your time...

—25—

If you suffer for doing what is right, God will reward you for
it. So don't worry or be afraid of threats. Instead, you must
worship Christ as Lord of your life. And if someone asks
about your Christian hope, always be ready to explain it.
—*1 Peter 3:15 (NLT)*

D id you know that God will place you in challenging
situations so you can share His Good News? (Read
Philippians 1:12)

A few years back God used the uncomfortable experience of
being virtually trapped on an Air India flight that was broken
down on the tarmac in Bangkok to place me right next to
a Hungarian Jew who happened to look like the photos of
Albert Einstein I had seen. The bushy eyebrows and wild hair
in mid-explosion accentuated the seventy odd years of deeply
entrenched lines creasing his face and forehead. He was, of
course, a physicist and an electrical engineer. Our unavoidable
first session lasted five eternal hours in a packed to the brim 747.
It was hot, humid and the air seemed heavy and suffocating. Just
when I thought it could not be more miserable, the flight deck
officer thought it would be a grand idea to offer the masses free
alcoholic drinks to offset the reality of our predicament.

Knowledge has weight and substance, at least in my mind it
does, and I knew that Air India had already chalked up twenty-
five near misses with other aircraft and one mid-air collision
that year, all because their pilots and air traffic controllers

didn't speak the same language dialect. Communication 101 says you have to understand each other's language in order to communicate.

Here I was stuck, imprisoned and unable to escape the very thing I had believed would carry me to my destination, an airplane that could not fly. Amidst the chaos I turned to my seat companion and said, "Hi, where are you headed?" That one question initiated a conversation that contained enough information to write a geo-political and physics textbook.

He wasn't shy about talking or telling me how he had escaped from Hungary in the early 1940s as Germany and Russia were rattling their sabers and struggling over eastern Europe like two wild dogs pulling at the same piece of meat. He eventually made his way to America, where, in his words, he had worked on the "early development of the crystal triode." Within moments I was whisked into a crash course in aeronautical science, physics and history.

I was his student. He told me about Russia and Germany's early work on the transistor's forerunners. How Pickard had patented the crystal detector back in 1906. He waved his arms as he told me about coming to America and how the crystal transistor led to a communications revolution. He drew elaborate pictures of jet turbine engines and described how kinetic energy is converted to mechanical power as high-pressure air is fed into the combustion chamber, as more and more passengers became loud and raucous over their drinks and arguments.

I listened, trying to grasp the concept of how fuel and air mixed and burned, providing high-pressure gases to drive the turbine. He pointed out that this kind of thermodynamic energy has basically four stages with minor variations. Somewhere between the compressor stage and the exhaust stage, he noticed the Star of David on my arm.

We shifted gears in our communication to the moral realm and we talked about the Nazi's homicidal solution to the "Jewish problem" in Europe and how many of his family and friends and neighbors had been murdered in concentration camps.

I was praying that God would open a door for me to talk to him about Christ and eternal life, as I asked him, *"What is it that drives men to do either good or evil?"* He had been down so called philosophy's road before and as he glared at me through his bushy eyebrows and stated that he emphatically did not believe God existed, if that was where I was taking the conversation. Then stated before I could respond, *"Religion is a fantasy that man invented to comfort himself."*

The mood slowed to a creeping crawl at that point. After what seemed like infinity, I asked him where he was going to teach in India. He informed me with his thick Hungarian accent that every year for the past thirty-two years he "traveled at his own expense" to New Deli where he lectured and taught electrical engineering students for three months. I explained to him that I saw his life as fascinating, going over what he had said and shown me in the previous four hours; how he was involved in the development of the crystal transistor, how he had explained and drew almost with blue print precision a jet turbine engine, that he, in fact, was an artist and that his creativity had to come from somewhere.

I pressed him once more into the moral sphere asking, "Why are you motivated to travel to India and pay your own expenses to teach these electrical engineering students every year?" His answer set me back a bit as he responded with force and animation. *"Because their brain is no larger than a walnut!"*

After composing myself, I said, "Okay, you do this because you are smarter than they are. That is obvious because you are the teacher and they are the students. But let me ask you this, as a teacher do you have a thought in your head?" He looked at me and his eyes narrowed, "Why, of course, why do you ask?" I responded, "Because I cannot see your thoughts. Obviously you are a brilliant man, however it is not until you speak or draw a picture or describe some concept or principle, do I know that you have a thought process. Even the most skilled neurosurgeon searching through your gray matter could only point out, this is where thought processes originate in the brain, but he could not show me one thought you have ever had. In the same way, just because I cannot show you Creator God, I can show you His creative genius and artistry everywhere and in some form in every human being. Your talents and gifts are indicators of a grand designer, a creator."

He scoffed at me but I pressed on and continued, "In these few hours you have brilliantly described how science and physics partnered in the beginning of all things. What I want to ask you is what about the ending? Can you tell me, do you know what will happen to you, to us when we die?"

For the first time in our conversation he was speechless and stammered as he sidestepped my pointed question. With timed accuracy I heard the captain inform us that Air India was going to place us in a hotel for the night and our flight to Bombay would resume tomorrow. My new friend gave me his business card and told me that he would give serious consideration to what I had shared with him. I shook his hand and prayed for him with a smile. My five hours of miserable delay was indeed a divine appointment.

Knowing, therefore, the terror of the Lord, we persuade men.
(2 Corinthians 5:11, KJV)

—26—

God told them, "I've never quit loving you and never will.
Expect love, love, and more love!"
—Jeremiah 31:3 (MSG)

To say "I love you" -- and really mean it -- takes courage. Love allows for no strings attached with expectations. No strings at all? None, nada, zip, zero. Have you noticed how some people struggle with the words *I love you?* You will frequently hear people use the generic version (or the readers digest version, as I call it): "Love you."

I'm not making an accusation, but rather thinking through and wrestling with my own inhibitions to simply say, *I love you.* Others implement the corporate version, the collective, "We love you." Both responses, "love you" and "we love you," are really defense mechanisms and attempts at protecting (I). For in love, it is the (I) that gets hurt, disappointed, and rejected. "Love you" is absent of commitment and "We love you" provides safety in numbers.

But (I) stands alone. *I love you* takes guts to say, if you really mean it. It's not something one can merely rush over as you go through the drive through of relationships. I certainly understand our human reluctance to avoid the words *I love you.* We may not feel the love, which causes us to drag our feet a little when it comes to "going on record" with those words.

Now don't get me wrong. I will *take* "love you" or "we love you" when those words are offered. It's better than saying, "I *don't* love you." And it's better than silence, any day. "I don't love you" at least lets me know where I stand. "Love you" gives me some hope that somebody, somewhere loves me, and "we love you," forewarns me that a group hug looms just ahead.

Silence, however, is no man's land.

Each year Jesus' Passion Week compels me to think deeply about these relationship dynamics. Jesus had guts. He was not silent. He did not leave people wondering. No guesswork here; no unfilled blanks, or dots left unconnected. He said it and lived it loud and clear, and a more courageous man you cannot find in all of history. He did not damn the world; He blessed the world with an iron act of His will to love even the unloving.

John captures the essence of His actions in John 13:1, "He loved them to the very end."

Jesus did not leave us wondering, and we don't want to leave this world with those we love wondering either, do we?

P.S. If you're wondering what God's love looks like, carefully go over 1 Corinthians 13. His fingerprints are all over the page.

—27—

*You let the distress bring you to God, not drive you from him. The result was all gain, no loss. Distress that drives us to God does that. It turns us around. It gets us back in the way of salvation. We never regret that kind of pain. But those who let distress drive them away from God are full of regrets, end up on a deathbed of regrets. *
—2 Corinthians 7:9-10 (MSG)

The first time I met him I was struck with his outdoor persona. He was a walking trademark for Remington or Winchester. He fit all the stereotypes I could conjure up, about a man living in the mountains, which he did.

His face was handsome, chiseled to square cut and weathered bronze for his less than fifty years of life. Little gray hair was visible, however, he didn't strike me as a man who would care about such things. I took notice of his ability to move effortlessly, with a steadiness of discipline and care. He oozed a ruggedness that was intimidating. He had presence.

As a wildlife officer, his state also commissioned him as a law enforcement officer. His Glock 9mm was positioned on his lean waist for instant action. His right hand was never far from his side. One look at this man and you knew he had what it takes. He had a quick smile yet there was something I noted deep in his eyes that meant business. All of my dealings with him, the talks we had shared, told me this man has a solid constitution; he had it inside and out.

Now, three years later, this personification of the independent, rugged, outdoor man is a quadriplegic, unable to move any part or portion of his body from the neck down. A permanent catheter allows him to exit body waste but he is not sure if and when that happens. He can breathe on his own but not much more.

It shocks me when I think about the sad fact that he will never ride another horse above the tree line, feeling the leather of the saddle or smell wood smoke at 10,000 feet, as an aspen fire crackles its warmth. He will never hear the cry of a bald eagle, catching warm air currents over a remote mountain lake in the wilderness, or a blue jay chattering away over some disagreement with a squirrel. He will never again feel the weight of a good rifle in his hands or the swing of a double bit ax, as it hits the mark. There will never be another opportunity to stand beside his two sons, shoulder to shoulder sharing a sunset as it washes a high mountain peak, in a last fleeting hurrah. No more feeling the delicate touch of a brook trout nudging a dry fly as it rises in an eddy, telegraphing a sudden strike which will split the water with churning energy and anticipated combat. There will not be another tender moment to caress his wife's face with his two strong hands or hold her tight in times of testing. For the rest of his life he will ponder his decision that changed all the possibilities of doing all the things he loved and was created to do with people who loved him and believed in him.

Somewhere along the line he changed course and took a different path. I can't say why because I don't know why. What I do know is that it seemed right to him to begin an affair with a younger woman. After all, a man reaching fifty and still turning a woman's head, especially a younger woman, is not to be taken lightly. It seemed right for him to move out of the house, leaving his wife and two sons behind in the stinging wake of immeasurable pain. It seemed right to him to abandon everything he had counted dear and precious. And ten months ago, it seemed right when he crawled into the pickup with his new love, driving from town, back down the river road to their ranch house. But something went wrong, something not expected, planned or anticipated. It didn't seem right when she screamed, as she lost control of the pickup, causing a terrible crash. *No, it just didn't feel right, worse than that, there is no feeling at all because his neck was broken in two places.*

Now isolated in a room with four walls, demanding constant care he has all the time in the world to think about the path he took and what might have been.

It just doesn't seem right.

> There is a path before each person that seems right,
> but it ends in death. (Proverbs 14:12, NLT).

—28—

*This has all been pioneer work, bringing the Message only into
those places where Jesus was not yet known and worshiped. My
text has been, Those who were never told of Him, they'll see Him!
Those who've never heard of Him, they'll get the Message!*
—Romans 15:19-21 (MSG)

Let me introduce you to Jack. I had the exciting honor of
baptizing Jack in water, salt water to be exact. Well... salt
water in the gulf of Thailand to be precise. Here is Jack's
story. Born into a Thai family with deep and long generational
Buddhist roots, Jack was raised in southern Thailand, near the
border of Malaysia.

His grandfather had purchased great tracks of land and now
his family farmed pineapple, coconut, rice, and even had large
rubber tree plantations.

Jack on the other hand was a schoolteacher, as was his wife.
Jack loved to joke around and have fun. In fact, he had gained
a reputation in the area as somewhat of a playboy. Jack really
liked to gamble and it caused his wife and family a lot of trouble
and much grief.

When I flew into the airport at Had Yai, Jack picked me up
in the midst of tight security because Muslim terrorists had
recently bombed the airport and are routinely causing the Thai
government internal problems in the region. Jack didn't seem
to be bothered by the terrorist tension in the region but as
we drove around the huge fresh water lake called Songkla, I

learned that Jack was experiencing internal family conflict and behind the scenes, under the surface, silently and seemingly unnoticed the Holy Spirit was at work in Jack's heart. In the past year his wife had been suffering from cancer. At the same time one of his two sons was diagnosed with leukemia. Jack's world began to unravel.

This prompted Jack to reevaluate his life. For 20 years he had taught school near his home. He quit his job and began to take care of his wife and son full time. His family said it was a huge change for him. As Jack and I, along with a few other family members, finished a long day of travel and survey of the area, none knew that Jack was about to experience a Holy Spirit orchestrated encounter with Jesus; much like the Ethiopian eunuch of Acts 8. We checked into our rooms and no doubt some would say by chance or coincidence, that one of our rooms contained a frayed and used copy of a Thai-English New Testament placed by the Gideon's. The first thing you need to know about this fact is that none of the other rooms in the hotel had a Gideon Bible, nor did the hotel know what the Bible was or where it came from, because I asked them about it.

That night before Jack went to sleep, his aunt, the only believer in this family of Buddhists, prayed with Jack to receive Christ as his saving God. The next morning at breakfast I learned about this and was able to explain more about his decision to follow Jesus. During our conversation, one of the hotel staff brought the blue book (Gideon Bible) and asked us to take it as they had no use for it. As I explained more of Jesus to Jack, his aunt and I presented him with the Bible. "Lord, that was great timing!"

Along the lines of our conversation, he said, "I need a new name!" His aunt asked him, "What name would you want to have?" He replied rather quickly with "Jack! I want to be called Jack."

Jack took his gift of a Bible, his new name and responded to my question about water baptism and said, "I want to be baptized like Jesus."

A few minutes later Jack and I waded into the warm, salty waters of the gulf of Thailand where I took his Bible and read Matthew 3:13 and Matthew 28:18-20 to him in English, then he read it in Thai.

And I said, "Jack, because of your confession of faith in Jesus, I baptize you in the name of the Father, and of the Son and of the Holy Spirit." Jack was all smiles when he came up out of the water and so was I.

—29—

Be quick to listen and slow to speak.
—James 1:19-20, (NLT)

I miss John Wayne. People born after 1979 may not even know who John Wayne was. An American icon, some would say, but I believe for all his fame and worldwide notoriety, he was a man of conviction. His quotes are some of my favorites, like: "Courage is being scared to death -- but saddling up anyway." And "Talk low, talk slow, and don't talk too much." Another way he said that was, "You're all hat and no boots."

In other words, long on talk and short on walk. He was pointing those of us who care to learn and practice to the art of listening. It seems like we are on talk overload these days. At any given time of the day you can turn on the TV or radio and find some expert talking. Not much listening though.

James had something to say about this point and he made it precise when he wrote, "Listening is an art that is crafted and learned over the course of time. It is forged in the classroom of uninterrupted solitude and silence and requires a humility that understands, I don't always have to be right and I don't always have to speak." Unless of course the sage was accurate when he wrote, "There is no sound sweeter than the sound of my own voice."

Years ago, I read and followed the wise counsel of a retiring corporate executive who said, "Son, you are going to have a thousand opportunities to keep your mouth shut. Take advantage of every one of them."

Sometimes I have been successful in pulling that off and never regretted taking the route of listening rather than speaking. Other times I have opened my mouth at the wrong time saying the wrong thing for the wrong reasons and I always walked away smaller in the end; both ends for sure.

Solomon was on to something when he wrote, "Even fools are thought to be wise when they keep silent; when they keep their mouths shut, they seem intelligent." (Proverbs 17:28, NLT).

Hmmm...

—30—

Let us run with patience the particular race that God has set before us.
—Hebrews 12:1 (TLB)

Travel has become a constant in our lives with conferences and speaking engagements around the country. One of my goals is to try and run wherever I find myself, both to see the area and keep fit. It is always a welcome relief to return home and sometimes I get to run a trail with one of my friends.

One spring day my friend, Larry Libby, and I took the dog, Eli Sackett, out for a couple hours run over the ridge of Badger Mountain, looping back on a trail that paralleled the Yakima River. The wind was fierce and I do mean all six letters F-I-E-R-C-E. At one point, on the south side of the ridge it was all we could do to stay on the trail.

As Larry and I ran together, I saw a picture in my mind concerning leadership as we traversed that ridge. There is a tension in trail running much like there is in leading. I am speaking specifically about leading and following. The man or woman out front has the tension of setting the pace just enough to take those following to another degree or two up and out on the exertion scale.

If the leader goes out too fast or sets the pace too fast, the followers often cannot keep up and lag behind. The follower on the other hand manages the tension of digging a little deeper to follow the leader. If you can at least keep that front guy in sight it fuels your fire to hang in there and press on.

If the follower is apathetic and refuses to tax their present ability then they will invariably drop behind and perhaps drop out. The tension is essential as the leader steps up the pace in measured and calculated degrees to stretch the team, company, church or business a little more yet not leave them in the dust just because you are the leader.

Larry, Eli and I stretched out, pressed against the fierce, resisting wind, which tested all of us; but we finished together. That is precisely what God has in mind. I believe it was what Paul meant when he wrote, "Follow me as I follow Christ."

In this way, the tension is a gift... not a grind.

—31—

"The thief's purpose is to steal, kill and destroy.
My purpose is to give life in all its fullness."
—*John 10:10, (TLB)*

I was cruising down a sandy trail one time, when I came across a mouse. There are a lot of mice traipsing around the desert area so don't think this is a rare or unusual sight, among the sagebrush landscape.

But this mouse was dead. Now, that isn't all that strange either. The truth is mice die. This mouse seemed to finish his race about half way across the trail I was on. I don't know why he died. It could have been his time or it could have been a bad decision on his part. In any event, he was indeed dead.

What caught my attention was a question scrolling across my mind, *Why hasn't a snake eaten that mouse yet?* It was surreal as the words scrolled over my brain waves as if I was watching a marquee while sipping iced mint tea in the shade. Right on the heels of this odd question was another scrolling marquee with this statement, *Because snakes will not eat dead creatures.* I knew that fact however this time the Holy Spirit was making a point for me to learn from.

He continued with the lesson, "What is it that attracts predators? What triggers their predatory nature to strike and kill?"

Before I could respond, He did with one word. "Life" the Holy Spirit whispered, "Predators are attracted to life. They care nothing for dead things. Life is what they are after." I got it.

Have you ever said or heard anyone say, "Why do I keep getting attacked? Why do I frequently feel assaulted?" Then thoughts like, "What's wrong with me?" and "What have I done wrong?" enter the picture attempting to stimulate more doubt and discouragement.

It is the life of God in you that the devil is attracted to. (see John 10) It triggers his predatory instinct. It is his nature to zero in and attempt to take the life out of you. Learn like I did from a dead mouse.

Better the mouse than you or me.

—32—

"Roll your works upon the Lord [commit and trust them wholly to Him; He will cause your thoughts to become agreeable to His will, and] so shall your plans be established and succeed."
Proverbs 16:3 (AMP)

Rivulets of sweat ran down my face and neck, magnifying the humidity. Weighing in at two-and-a-quarter pounds, my World-War-Two-vintage steel pot helmet felt more like a head-shaped oven, baking my brain rather than protecting it.

With twenty-seven other men in my platoon, I was standing at attention in the hot afternoon sun, doing my best to concentrate as our drill sergeant gave specific instructions about our combat boots.

The story I'm about to share with you is true. I was there, making a plan, working the plan, yet I missed the mark and paid for it.

Sometimes we miss the mark, don't we? We do our best to aim for the bull's eye, take our best shot, and then find out that we were way, *way* off.

In our second week of Army boot camp training at Fort Knox, Kentucky, reality was beginning to settle into the cracks and crevices of my soul. Life was taking on new meaning as we stood at attention in front of our DI (Drill Instructor) or Drill Sergeant.

For no good reason, one of the men in the first squad began to throw small rocks over his shoulder every time the DI looked down at the pair of boots he was using as an example, threatening us with bodily harm if we didn't get it right.

The DI's Smokey Bear hat, designed with a wide brim 360 degrees around the crown, blocked his field of vision every time he tilted his head down. That's when the funny guy in the front row would take a chance and chuck a rock.

With each toss someone—usually in the second or third squad—took a pelt in the face, neck, or upper body. Finally one of the rocks hit me. *That does it!* I thought. The next time the DI tilted his head, continuing to promise us his intense personal attention if anyone messed up, I squatted down and quickly grabbed a stone about the size of a quarter.

Zeroing in on the back of the assailant's neck, I waited for my moment like a hunter. When the DI looked down again, I threw the rock at our tormentor with a quick, sharp, whip of my right hand. My target was only four feet away, and I threw that rock as hard as I could.

At first, my aim looked true and accurate.

Then to my horror—like a fastball rising over home plate— the stone seemed to lift in the air, striking my nemesis on the side of his steel pot helmet.

And then it ricocheted.

The stone pinged off the helmet, flying like a missile and arching in a fantastic trajectory. Just as the DI raised his head to glare at us, the stone struck him squarely between the eyes. Well, the bridge of the nose would be more accurate. With a thump, the stone landed, then dropped to his leg and bounced back into the gravel.

Like a word spoken or a bullet fired, I could not retrieve that stone.

Instantly 28 backbones stiffened and 56 eyeballs grew twice their normal size. At first the DI acted as if nothing had happened, then with a number of expletives (including some I had never heard before), he demanded that the perpetrator turn himself in, now! *No way,* I told myself, as visions of my epitaph flashed in my head. So, with time honored skill, our DI began punishing the whole platoon with a rigorous workout. After several minutes, I got it. I could either face the DI now, or face the entire platoon later.

I confessed.

Did the DI throw me in the brig? No. Did I do pushups and sit ups for the rest of that miserable day? Yes, as a matter of fact, I did.

Ecclesiastes 3:5 says there is "A time to throw stones and a time to gather stones." This was *not* the time to throw a stone, believe me. Were there consequences to my ill thought out plan? You bet!

I learned a valuable lesson that day. Pray, think ahead, pray some more, and commit your plans to the Lord.

Or prepare to pay the price.

—33—

Without oxen a stable stays clean, but you
need a strong ox for a large harvest.
—Proverbs 14:4 (NLT)

I clearly remember the first time the Holy Spirit illuminated my heart with this scripture. I was flying to Dallas, Texas, to an International gathering of believers in August 1984.

Vivid memories of my boyhood, filled my mind.... "Son, clean out those stalls in the barn today!" My dad gave those instructions often, after all, we lived on a farm along the Columbia River and cleaning out the barn stalls was part of the reward of milk and beef farming. No, I didn't think like that back then. All I knew was that I was ankle deep in manure with a scoop shovel.

My memories crystallized as I read the verse again on that flight to Texas. The Holy Spirit whispered words I understood and have kept close to my heart since that day, "No manure, no milk; no milk, no manure." I know what you're thinking, "Just go to the store and reach into the dairy case and pull out a clean, neat, fresh gallon of milk and no mess." I don't believe that is what Solomon had in mind when he wrote these words. And of course, it may work today for a glass of milk in America, but it has never worked for an effective ministry.

Nancy and I were two years into our first pastorate. My idealism had already taken some painful blows with the fact that "ministry is messy!" and "sometimes it stinks." And it is also the most fulfilling, life-giving endeavor you could ever give yourself too.

Think about Jesus, please. When Jesus arrived on planet earth, He was born in a very unexpected spot -- something comparable to a barn, Middle Eastern style. His first bassinet was in a manger -- nothing more than an ox, sheep, goat and donkey, feeding trough. (Mmm, that makes sense).

A barn was filled with goats and oxen and other livestock. Can you smell it? It is filled with the pungent odors of livestock, including most noticeably, dung and urine from the animals.

"Without oxen, the manger is clean." What is this really saying? It could be God's word for you today, " In order for Jesus to be present in ministry, we must welcome the messiness that demands to be cleaned up."

Look at it this way; Jesus rolled up his sleeves, put on knee-high rubber boots, grabbed a scoop shovel and waded into humanities sinful, stinking mess. He works especially well in the messy things in my life. From these messes comes an abundant harvest. God has always found fertile soil in people who gave their messes to Him for cleanup. The pattern can be seen repeatedly by those He used most in the Bible.

Father God is filled with paradoxes and so is His kingdom.

Why can't life be seamless and smooth like that jug of milk in the dairy case? Look at Jesus' response to the religious elite concerning His stall-cleaning mission. Jesus, overhearing, shot back, "Who needs a doctor: the healthy or the sick? Go figure out what this Scripture means: 'I'm after mercy, not religion.' I'm here to invite outsiders, not coddle insiders." (See Matthew 9:10-13, in the *Message*)

Jesus, from His birth, has always showed up in the messes of life to write a message of God's love and truth. This is what brings us into a season of large harvest.

The bigger the mess in your stall, the bigger the harvest. God works in barns, stalls and feeding mangers, so come on…. grab a shovel!

—34—

So here's what I think: The best thing you can do right now is to finish
what you started last year and not let those
good intentions grow stale."
—2 Corinthians 8:10 (MSG)

Okay it's no secret, surprise or shock. Men are typically task driven. I am no exception. We find value in accomplishment and we want people to know we are self-reliant and proactive, a "get 'er done" breed of man. Herein enters the dilemma. When you mix "task driven" with "self reliance" you end up with a creature that highly resists doing things like walking up to somebody they don't know and asking for directions or calling someone they know and saying, "I need help."

I'll meander in a grocery store for fifteen minutes trying to find Arborio rice or red pepper flakes on my own because accomplishing the task isn't going to be satisfying unless I can do it on my own.

Like most men, I focus on the goal. In other words, what's the bottom line and how can I overcome the obstacles to reach the objective, take the hill, and conquer the opposition? Well, I reached a goal, completed a task, and overcame an obstacle, but it wasn't because I was self-reliant, goal-oriented or task-driven.

I reached the goal because of God's grace and the generosity of a friend. And it was a sweet victory. Let me tell you about it. For a good number of years, wherever I happen to be, I will climb all the surrounding mountain or hilltops and pray over the region. This is something I've been doing in the Pacific Northwest of our nation -- and over other nations as well -- for many years.

In the Columbia Basin of southeast Washington State, it wasn't long before I had ascended all the hilltops in the area, with one menacing exception, Rattle Snake Mountain. The western USA has some impressive and high peaks, so Rattlesnake Mountain isn't that high as far a mountains go out west, only about 3,200 feet. Further it's closed to the public and has been since the Manhattan Project of WWII.

From every other inferior hill in our region, I would look to the west of Rattle Snake calculating how I would master its forbidden slopes. Every door I knocked on said "no."

But God does things in ways we men can rarely wrap our heads around, if ever. When I received the invitation to join a small group of people on top of Rattle Snake Mountain, I almost missed it. I didn't get it initially because I did not recognize what God was up to. Why? Because this time it was not according to my presupposed thinking or experience.

I did not run to the top, I went as a guest with a friend where we joined about a dozen other people to visit the observatory on top of the mountain. Our host was a geologist and an astronomer. After a short and compelling talk, a stringed quartet from the local stringed symphony, filled the air and the observatory with the beautiful sounds of Haydn, Mozart and Schubert. As they played, and the guests were taking a view through the telescope, I slipped out into the dark and prayer walked around the top of that windy summit. I could see the entire eighty mile Yakima valley lit up to the south and west, the Hanford site to the north, Tri-Cities and Walla Walla to the east.

It was a compelling experience to pray for the region, as my prayers seemed to be carried by the wind and the Holy Spirit. This completes my goal of praying atop every high point in our valley.

The apostle Paul stimulated the capable believers in Corinth when he wrote: "Your heart's been in the right place all along. You've got what it takes to finish it up, so go to it. Once the commitment is clear, you do what you can, not what you can't. The heart regulates the hands" (2 Corinthians 8:10-12).

Okay, what's the bottom line? When God gives you a directive, do what you can and when you hit an impasse, trust Him to pull it off His way, in His time.

—35—

Don't shuffle along, eyes to the ground, absorbed with the things right
in front of you. Look up, and be alert to what is going on around
Christ— that's where the action is. See things from His perspective.
—Colossians 3:2 (MSG)

Standing on the edge of a canyon not far from the 12,000-
foot peak of Mount Adams, in south central Washington
State was a surreal experience for me. A light mist fell
across the face and shoulders of the mountain on which I stood.
As I took in the view, it appeared that God had slipped into the
canyon under the cover of darkness and with a child-like joy had
skipped over the mountains with cans of scarlet red, and sunset
gold paint, splashed the trees and under brush with brilliant
hues, left then right, with random, wild and unrestrained slings
of His celestial paint brush. I can't tell you with words how
stunningly beautiful this autumn moment really was. I wish I
could bottle it for you.

I inhaled, even absorbed the air, then imbibed the mood
and the atmosphere, as I relaxed and exhaled slowly, feeling
very alive.

I felt the smile of God. He washed me with a fresh perspective;
compressed into my soul an above ground view. I am not talking
about an out of body experience, but rather the capacity to
see upward, not downward -- the ability to increase spiritual
altitude, thus adjusting mental attitude.

Standing on the lip of that canyon (I'm not kidding), it seemed like the mountains shrugged their massive shoulders, chuckling in God's presence and saying, "So what! Rise above it!" Jesus did.

Yes, He did and with skill and style and substance. He did not live under pressure or by pressure. He rose above it all, the vilifications, the attacks, the setbacks, the insults, and the opposition. Do you know what else? He was not small souled about it either. He did not blame His dad, or His friends, or the economy or the competition. He rose above it all. When I breathed in that high altitude air, I breathed in God-colors, God-flavors, and God's attitude.

Leaders must climb mountains sometimes to see a different perspective, to rise above the controversies, jealousies, pettiness and smallness of soul in order to accomplish anything worthwhile, anything that will last. Jesus climbed a mountain, which has changed many altitudes and attitudes. As I recollect, that mountain is called Mount Calvary.

Now exhale.

—36—

No one abuses his own body, does he? No, he feeds and pampers
it. That's how Christ treats us, the church, since we are part of
his body. And this is why a man leaves father and mother and
cherishes his wife. No longer two, they become "one flesh." This is
a huge mystery, and I don't pretend to understand it all. What is
clearest to me is the way Christ treats the church. And this provides
a good picture of how each husband is to treat his wife, loving
himself in loving her, and how each wife is to honor her husband.
—Ephesians 5:29-33 (MSG)

D ust swirled around our feet as we dropped off the peak
of Badger Mountain for the second time in two hours.
Intense, autumn sun pressed down on us with unrelenting
heat, and I was hot, sweaty, covered with dust and tired.

As we navigated the first switchback, Ben at my side, glanced
my way and said, "Micah, I have a question for you."

"Okay," I said.

"I would like to ask your permission to marry your daughter."

"Ahhh, Hannah?" I said as I coughed several times,
attempting to convince him that the steep trail dropping away
in sharper angles and degrees was the cause.

My thoughts swept back to a mountain slope in central
Oregon in 2004. On that day, another young man, Gareth
-- now married to my oldest daughter, Andrea, requested my
permission to ask her to marry him.

Truly, I *am* a blessed man for having only two daughters, Andrea and Hannah -- beautiful inside and out -- that they would court such men who would honor the Lord, honor them, and honor me with this kind of request. It is unusually admirable in today's culture. I'm not certain I could take this kind of news on many more mountaintops!

People look at romance, marriage, and life thorough a variety of lenses these days. One of my favorite landing spots in our local paper is the "Dear Judy" section, where folks write in, hoping to find solutions to their dilemmas. It's something of a down-home "Dear Abby" column, with most of the letters centered on romance and marriage.

Here are two examples from last month:

Dear Judy,

The man I'm engaged to is extremely considerate, and when it comes to my parents, he is genuinely concerned about their welfare, their interests and finances. He's a wonderful provider and I feel fortunate to have met him and that we are planning a life together. But I am having problems handling a couple of habits he has, and I don't know what to do. No matter where we go to eat, whenever food is brought to our table he sniffs the entire contents of each plate, even if it is brought to someone else. If it's good, he strikes the table with his fist and yells, "Go, Lakers!" If he thinks the aroma is bad, he screams, "In the penalty box!" How would you handle this?

—Food Fighter

Dear Food Fighter:

Don't eat out until this guy is housebroken. Put him on a leash and jerk him back when he sniffs the food. As far as yelling out, "Go, Lakers!" or "In the penalty box," I'd put a muzzle on this guy.

Dear Judy,

I've been dating an attractive and very generous man for the last six weeks. He is very attentive and caring, and everything is going okay. However, on all of our dates so far, we always go to Wal-Mart. Sometimes we don't even buy things. We just stroll the aisles hand-in-hand while he whistles, "I've been working on the railroad." Do you think something is wrong with this? I don't want to hurt his feelings, but what is the proper protocol for suggesting going on dates that don't involve going to Wal-Mart?

—Bored Shopper

Dear Bored Shopper:

Shop one more time with him at Wal-Mart, purchase a huge train set, put it up in his home and let him whistle away "I've been working on the railroad" until he's blue in the face. And for heaven sakes, keep your dates "on track" somewhere else than Wal-Mart.

With all of these things whirling through my mind -- Gareth's first mountain request in central Oregon, and Ben's request on Badger Mountain, coupled with Mr. Go Lakers and I've been working on the railroad -- I snapped back to reality just in time to catch myself where the trail disappeared under my feet.

Getting back on the path and back in my stride, I continued on down the mountain with Ben, who had my full attention... and my full blessing to ask Hannah to marry him.

—37—

Then the man of God went to the king of Israel and said, "This is what the LORD says: 'The Arameans have said, "The LORD is a god of the hills and not of the valleys." So I will defeat this vast army for you. Then you will know that I am the LORD.'"
—1 Kings 20:28 (NLT)

I have a penchant for mountaintops. The view is always incredible and I never descend without a brand new perspective. Some folks adore penthouses, but give me a pointed pinnacle of terra firma any day. Talk about a room with a view.

This is fresh on my mind you see, because I recently climbed one such mountain in the Colorado Rockies. Money could not buy what I experienced in my soul from that thin-air vantage point. Admittedly, mountain climbing is a tough task and downright demanding. At times it is without mercy and unforgiving, because beauty and terror can travel together. Is it worth it? You bet it is.

However, I have come to realize that God didn't make mountaintops for living on, but learning from. They are the consummate teachers about life. Sometimes life is experienced on the vistas of clear vision and perpetual hopes and dreams. Other times it feels like life is blanketed by fog, where vision is pushed back and hopes are thickly layered with disappointments. The Arameans mentioned in 1 Kings 20 were obviously not God-followers, given their assumption that He only hung out on mountain tops and not down in the valleys. Their presumption became their undoing, because He is LORD of high and low places alike.

If you think about it, living on a perpetual mountaintop is a harsh environment where the wind can be violent and sweet scented flowers rarely have time to bloom. On the other hand, I've been in valleys where the sun has little chance to shine and the mist obscures vision and clouds perspective. If you walk far enough, you will summit mountains and eventually drop down into valleys. Mountains and valleys both have something to offer you. The same is true in life.

Whether you find yourself on the high vista of a mountaintop today, or in a low place called a valley, Jesus is with you, so keep walking.

—38—

But Peter and John replied,
"Do you think God wants us to obey you rather than Him?"
—Acts 4:19-20 (NLT)

The older I get the less I know. Twenty-five years ago I had more answers than I do now. I was more rigid and religious and self-righteous. After a quarter century of being hammered on the anvil of life, however, I now find things to be much less simplistic and certain.

A Persian proverb says, "He who knows not, and knows not that he knows not is a fool; shun him. He who knows not, and knows that he knows not, is a child; teach him. He who knows, and knows not that he knows, is asleep; wake him. He who knows, and knows that he knows, is wise; follow him."

This is what I know, Jesus said, "Let Me tell you why you are here. You're here to be salt-seasoning that brings out the God-flavors of this earth. If you lose your saltiness, how will people taste godliness? You've lost your usefulness and will end up in the garbage. Here's another way to put it: You're here to be light, bringing out the God-colors in the world. God is not a secret to be kept. We're going public with this, as public as a city on a hill. If I make you light-bearers, you don't think I'm going to hide you under a bucket, do you? I'm putting you on a light stand. Now that I've put you there on a hilltop, on a light stand... shine! Keep open house; be generous with your lives. By opening up to others, you'll prompt people to open up with God, this generous Father in heaven. Matthew 5:13-16, (MSG)

What do we do now? Good question. I like John Wesley's motto, *"Do all the good you can by all the means you can by all the ways you can in all the places you can and at all the times you can to all the people you can as long as you ever can."*

Go with what you *know!*

—39—

"The LORD has given me a strong warning not to think like everyone else does. He said, 'Don't call everything a conspiracy, like they do, and don't live in dread of what frightens them. Make the LORD of Heaven's Armies holy in your life. He is the one you should fear. He is the one who should make you tremble. He will keep you safe."
—Isaiah 8:11-14a. (NLT)

Yesterday, while praying for my children, the Holy Spirit massaged God's Word into my soul. These are words that have given me both courage and comfort through the years... and they are words I pray will comfort and encourage them and you as well.

On the one hand, there is a vast mountain range of reasons for God's people to slip into neutral (at best) or retreat (at worst). Should I recite the long list of economic, political, moral, and spiritual reasons that would incline us to quake with anxiety and worry? *I think not.*

Israel faced great dread before the inevitable Assyrian invasion. Isaiah chapter eight features a stream of negative news similar to what you might encounter from the Associated Press or CNN these days. Or any days, for that matter.

To tell the truth, God's Word is different. The Bible holds out strong warnings and even stronger promises to God's people. In the passage above, it's almost as if God is saying, "Isaiah, what in the world are you thinking? You're being swept along with the low-level opinions and fears of everyone around you, focusing on them and their reactions to impending danger."

May I continue to extract what I believe God is saying to His people in any crisis? "Don't allow yourself to imagine that the madness of the masses and the crisis of the moment have anything to do with dictating, driving, or determining who I AM and what I AM doing."

Slowly and prayerfully, reread the verses that begin this column. Now… are these difficult times? Yes, they are indeed. Does it appear we face amassed threats as never before? Yes, it certainly does.

But God is not shocked, awed, surprised, or rocking back on His heels.

Bottom line, He is saying, "Who will you allow to write the scripts for your lives? Who will compose the plot line and the conclusion? Someone will. And you get to decide who that will be."

That's worth thinking over.

—40—

Let the peace of Christ keep you in tune with each other, in step
with each other. None of this going off and doing your own
thing. And cultivate thankfulness. Let the Word of Christ—
Message—have the run of the house. Give it plenty of room in
your lives. Instruct and direct one another using good common
sense. And sing, sing your hearts out to God! Let every detail in
your lives—words, actions, whatever—be done in the name of the
Master, Jesus, thanking God the Father every step of the way.
—Colossians 3:16 (MSG)

*O*ikos is a Greek word for "house." Your *oikos* is the sphere
of your relationships, which includes family and friends
but may also include the businesses you frequent, and
your place of employment. It takes in your employer, colleagues,
coworkers, neighbors, and associates.

Oikos is formed through close human ties and relationships.
In other words, it is your circle of relationships in your world
and in your life. We pray for our *oikos*.

Nancy and I want you to know that we are praying for you.
Each day we lift up family and friends, pastors and churches to
the Lord in prayer and intercession. We pray the prayer of faith
for those who are sick and struggling and we give thanks to Jesus
for the good reports we receive.

We let miracles happen by never giving up on God's faithful
activity behind the scenes. God's work in our lives -- though
often subtle, silent, and out of the spotlight -- never stops, day or

night. His ultimate intention and the great desire of His Father-heart is to bless you beyond your wildest dreams, thoughts, or imaginations.

Yes, we may very well find ourselves facing some difficult days ahead in our nation… days that will confront our courage and circumstances, that will challenge and test our faith. However, the Holy Spirit in you can handle all of them with resurrection energy and divine power.

Are you aware that the prophet Samuel believed it would be a sin against the Lord not to pray for those people close to you? See 1 Samuel 12:23.

We ask Father God to protect you.

"His huge outstretched arms protect you, under them you're perfectly safe; his arms fend off all harm. Fear nothing -- not wild wolves in the night, not flying arrows in the day, not disease that prowls through the darkness, not disaster that erupts at high noon" (Psalm 91:4-6).

"When you go through deep waters and great trouble, I will be with you. When you go through rivers of difficulty, you will not drown! When you walk through the fire of oppression, you will not be burned up; the flames will not consume you" (Isaiah 43:2, NLT).

"Do not be afraid or discouraged, for the LORD is the one who goes before you. He will be with you; he will neither fail you nor forsake you" (Deuteronomy 31:8, NLT).

We ask Father God to preserve you.

"The minute I said, 'I'm slipping, I'm falling,' your love, GOD, took hold and held me fast. When I was upset and beside myself, you calmed me down and cheered me up" (Psalm 94:19).

"The righteous do not fear bad news; they confidently trust the Lᴏʀᴅ to care for them. They are confident and fearless and can face their foes triumphantly" (Psalm 112:6-8, ɴʟᴛ).

We ask Father God to provide for you.

Jesus said, "Come to me, all of you who are weary and carry heavy burdens, and I will give you rest (Matthew 11:28, ɴʟᴛ).

And this same God who takes care of me will supply all your needs from his glorious riches, which have been given to us in Christ Jesus (Philippians 4:19, NLT).

—41—

Do your best, prepare for the worst,
then trust God to bring victory.
—Proverbs 21:31 (MSG)

I am not sure who was more surprised, they or I. I do know who was more embarrassed though and it was not I. They were. Well, you would be too if you were caught with your pants down.

This is a true story. Moving up a steep trail and one I had never run before I came over a rise with my dog Eli, and there they were twenty paces ahead, the man on the right side of the trail and the woman on the left; both with their pants down.

Now, if you have ever been caught with your pants down you know firsthand how embarrassing that can be.

Of course, they both moved faster than a centipede at a jitterbug contest when they saw me, pulling their drawers up and jumping back onto the trail as if nothing happened, although with red faces.

We walked up to them and acted as if nothing happened, asking about the trail system and making small talk. *Eli Sackett, the dog, was smiling at me.*

I noticed they would not make eye contact or look at me, because we all knew something had happened, which none of us were prepared for or expected in this chance meeting. Moments like this are em-bar-assing.

Most of us have a story or two about an embarrassing situation, where we felt as though our pants were down, even if they weren't. The proverbial idiom of getting caught with your pants down is common occurrence in the lives of the unprepared and unthinking. Ed Cole used to say frequently, "The man who thinks ahead is ahead of the man who doesn't." So true and so important to remember.

Jacob probably wished he had thought ahead before he was trapped by Laban's cunning.

Samson thoughtlessly laid his head in Delilah's lap.

David was shocked when Nathan said, "You are the man!"

Peter boasted of courageous commitment but ended up cursing.

The truth is, you don't have to be a Bible character, pop-celebrity or politician to get caught with your pants down, proverbial or not. You may merely be like two ordinary people who went for a hike and didn't take the time to go before they left the house.

I am sure they prepared better next time.

—42—

Pray for the peace of Jerusalem.
May all who love this city prosper.
—Psalm 122:6 (NLT)

My mom moved to Israel, landing in Tel Aviv on September 29, 2000, the day after PLO chairman Arafat declared the second Intifada against Israel.

She literally landed in the middle of war and a national crisis. She went to Israel to serve with "Bridges For Peace", a Christian organization dedicated to helping resettle Jews, making Aliyah. Yet, I am confident she was there to pray for the peace of Jerusalem, which she faithfully continues to do.

After her arrival, it was more than a week before she was able to call us. I felt a sense of relief when she finally called saying she was fine. As we talked on the phone, she could hear artillery fire in the distance. She informed me that Bridges for Peace had notified all their staff that they could return home because of the danger but mom would have none of that idea.

And she stayed for most of the next ten years, walking the streets of Jerusalem, praying for God's shalom to rest upon the land and the people. Like many others, mom modeled what Isaiah 62:6 announces,

> "O Jerusalem, I have posted watchmen on your walls; they will pray day and night, continually. Take no rest, all you who pray to the LORD." (NLT)

Many times, we've taken teams to Israel, and Mom would arrange for us to visit the Bridges for Peace food bank or other special people or sites. Her faith and love are always contagious. *What a wonderful example she is to us.*

Peace has not come to Israel yet. Perhaps, real peace will not arrive until the Prince of Peace arrives, and until then, like mom, may we all hear the summons to pray for the "peace of Jerusalem".

—43—

He was despised and rejected—a man of sorrows,
acquainted with bitterest grief. Yet it was our weaknesses He carried;
it was our sorrows that weighed Him down.
—Isaiah 53:3-4 (NLT)

Research scientists at the University of Virginia discovered that most people perceive a hill to be steeper than it really is, especially if they're tired and carrying a heavy load.

Test participants consistently misjudged the hill's slope, thinking a ten-degree slant was about thirty degrees and rating a five-degree slope at nearly twenty degrees. Most participants could not believe they were that far off.

The weaknesses and weights of life can fog our perceptions. Have you ever thought about your perception of Jesus? I have and it has prompted me to compare my perception with biblical revelation.

An old adage says, "God created man in His own image and man has been returning the favor ever since." I don't know about anyone else but I have found it rather easy to stereotype Jesus. Distracted by such notions as approaching Jesus as if He were something like an emergency first aid kit (Use only in case of disasters) as I pull Him off of the shelf when I have a crisis of some kind.

But really, what would it have been like to walk the dusty roads in Galilee and Judea observing in person the most extraordinary events ever to unfold in human history? Discovering who Jesus was, why He came, and what He left behind. Step by step, following Jesus on His mission and imbibing His Spirit. There have always been those of the religious persuasion that make it their aim to deconstruct Jesus.

From the crowd Luke quotes "…you say, 'Here is a glutton and a drunkard, a friend of tax collectors and "sinners" (Luke 7:34, NLT).

Not much has changed today, as groups like the "Jesus Seminar" seek to prove that the Bible is merely a human book and Jesus was nothing more than a religious worker. Nonetheless, it is because of the very observations the religious crowd made, that my heart resonates deeply toward Jesus. Do you see it? They called Him "a friend of sinners."

Jesus was not moved by opinion polls. They didn't matter then. They certainly don't matter today. The proof is in the pudding is what Jesus went on to say. Yes, every picture the Holy Spirit has given of Jesus enables us to see Him for who He is, God, King, Redeemer, Healer, Savior, Lord and Protector. The list is endless of how we perceive Jesus.

Notwithstanding, the one view of Jesus that has drawn more people to God than any other is the fact that Jesus loves people, especially the worst kind of sinners. He identified with those who were rejected by society. Jesus knew rejection Himself. His family thought Him insane, His community ran Him out of town, His closest companions betrayed, denied and abandoned Him, and His fellow citizens traded His life for that of a hard-core criminal. Jesus is well acquainted with the piercing sting of rejection.

No wonder, He highlights the last, least and the lost. Jesus loves people, especially the unlovely. Only God would think of that. Religion has always gone for the opulent and the impressive. Not Jesus. His ministry is marked by moving among the poor and rejected. He intentionally touched lepers, dined with the unclean, and forgave thieves, adulterers, and prostitutes.

Read Luke 7:35-44 from Eugene Peterson's "Message." My point is profoundly made in this beautiful picture of grace.

Now the hill doesn't seem so steep.

—44—

Then Simon Peter drew a sword and slashed off the right ear of
Malchus, the high priest's servant. But Jesus said to Peter,
"Put your sword back into its sheath."
—John 18:10-11, (NLT)

Have you ever met someone who always has his or her
sword unsheathed? I am not referring to the occasional
disagreement we all experience. But a chronic attitude
that says "let's fight!"

I have and I am saddened to admit that before I met Jesus,
it was true of me. So I know whereof I speak. I don't believe I
am alone in my fondness of the Apostle Peter. As I study the
earthiness of his life I find solace. Peter was real, no pretense
and no put-on. Although bold and courageous, you can feel
the cracks around the edges of his life as you read his story. He
doesn't easily hide his flaws (even after Pentecost, see Acts 10)
however he never slammed the door shut on Jesus, even in his
darkest hour. You see, Jesus never gave up on Peter.

John shares a powerful lesson from Peter's life. It is one we
can glean rich grace from. A lesson Peter would never forget.
And one that will help us live in peace. When Jesus commanded
him to sheath his sword he was placing His finger on Peter's
pulse. In a moment of anger most likely driven by fear, Peter
learned he was out of sync with Jesus. He had lost the Lord's
cadence and rhythm.

I don't believe for one minute that Jesus was advocating pacifism, as some would suggest. Rather, He was asking Peter and all of us for that matter, "Who are you warring against?"

No, He didn't use those specific words but the account bears that out. I will never forget the day several years ago when the Holy Spirit whispered into my heart, "Many people are weaklings when it comes to confronting and standing against evil but often hostile combatants when relating to people."

"What do You mean?" I asked the Lord. From that time until now, He continues to teach me what He meant by that simple word of wisdom. As one man wrote, "If Paul and Dan have a problem, and John and Dan have a problem, and Sally and Dan have a problem and Joe and Dan have a problem... then Dan is probably the problem. The issue is this. Who are you warring against and who are you allowing to beat you unmercifully?

Nothing less than a hellish plot which particularly victimizes leaders. The hardness of heart toward human beings is usually the result of a spirit of rejection that has found a foothold in one of Father God's dear ones.

Not more than a day spent with someone controlled by a combative spirit is required to see it in action. Their sword is rarely sheathed as they take on people both publicly and privately. It is a sad and broken scene to witness for they rarely see what others see.

And they wonder why no one comes around.

—45—

Don't worry about anything; instead, pray about everything.
Tell God what you need, and thank him for all he has done.
—Philippians 4:6, (NLT)

Worry creased my brow, but what bothered me more was the worry creasing my soul. "I am not a worrier, Lord, but I am concerned!" "We're leaving for southern Thailand in three days!"

"What do you want me to do with this report?"

In retrospect, a couple of essential things occur to me: one, Jesus knew exactly when we were leaving for southern Thailand, and two, the report didn't upset Him in the least. I had been reading the State Department's specific country warning for U.S. citizens *not* to travel to southern Thailand. And it had sparked a tinge of fear in my heart. Not a fear for myself in particular, but for the twelve other people -- including family members and children -- who would join me in this tense and volatile area.

Now, I was arguing with God, "The last time I flew to Hat Yai, the airport was bombed." I was concerned and I was complaining, which led to another Holy Spirit conviction and correction party. So, I repented and moved forward in faith once again.

God does not ask us to do foolish things or dumb things. He does, however, ask us to trust Him, and I settled that issue again as I had so many times in the past.

We checked with the U.S. Embassy in Thailand and flew to Hat Yai. The car I was riding in from the airport pulled up in front of the Samila Beach Hotel, and I couldn't believe what I was looking at as we came to a halt. In the front of the hotel and throughout the lobby several hundred Muslims were standing around. Our entire team had to walk through them to register for our rooms. Again, that old uneasy feeling gripped my gut as I pressed through to the desk.

I learned that an Islamic conference was convening for the next few days in our hotel with the theme, "Saudi Arabia." *Great,* I thought. Within the hour, some of the team was reporting to me that Muslims were questioning them in the elevators about who they were, where they were from, and what they were doing in southern Thailand.

That night at 9:40 p.m., seven bombs rocked the area -- one near our hotel on Samila Beach. The next day the *Bangkok Post* included this front page report; "Seven Bombs Rock Songkhla."

Okay, Lord, I prayed as we drove out to our first day of medical care, *we are in Your faithful hands, and we will do what You have called us to do down here.* Still, I was a bit relieved to see that we were provided a police escort and protection as we worked and provided medical care for hundreds of people.

I share that account because it was another lesson in God's protecting power and the kingdom principle of prayer and intercession that He has placed in the hands of His people. I am confident that God protected us from harm and danger as we ministered to one thousand people over the course of five days.

But protection and favor like that doesn't "just happen." God stepped in to shield us, and I believe He did it in direct response to the intercessions of His people on our behalf -- People standing in the gap for us -- People holding the other end of the lifeline. People who, through prayer and intercession, opened and held open the door to the kingdom where we were located, and held it open as long as we were in the room of service. *God covered our backs with His prayer force.*

When we returned to Bangkok, board members, George and Wendy Midbust and Joanne and Marv Erickson met with Global Gateway Network's Thai attorney. Sitting in a circle she looked at me and said, "Micah, there hasn't been any Islamic terrorist bombing in that area for a long time. Don't you think it's interesting that the bombings happened the very day you arrived in the area? I was praying for your team, and the Lord showed me that the enemy was angry because the kingdom of God had arrived."

Now, with a kingdom stake driven in the ground, I am relieved the mission was a success. Years ago, an aged church leader walked up to the pew where I was seated, and I will never forget what he said to me, "Son, just remember this in kingdom ministry. No battles, no victories."

—46—

Jacob woke up from his sleep. He said, "GOD is in this place, And I
didn't even know it!" He was terrified.
He whispered in awe, "This is the Gate of Heaven."
—Genesis 28:16-17 (MSG)

The view on top of Badger Mountain was obscured by a driving sleet traveling more horizontally than vertically. The temperature was bone penetrating cold and the wind was blowing so hard I had difficulty standing up right. My family had moved back to southeastern Washington at the end of 2000. The New Year was now a month old and thrashing it's way out of the long dark days of December. Early on I made it a habit of hiking to the top of one of the surrounding hills to pray.

As I staggered against the storm, I was second-guessing my decision on this particular day. When I tried to shield my eyes and face from the howling slivers of ice, I heard the Holy Spirit say, "Pray for your brothers and sisters!"

Somehow the prompt of the Spirit outgunned my wild surrounding and I spotted a large rock near the trail, right on top of the mountain. I went over and knelt down behind the rock, attempting to protect myself from the blast as much as I wanted to be obedient to the Spirit's summons.

After praying for each of my brothers and sisters I stood up and ran down the leeward side of the hill, glad to be moving again. Not many hours later I received a telephone call informing me that my sister, Ann, older than I, had unexpectedly died from a massive heart attack. I was shocked and saddened.

After her funeral service, I went back to the top of Badger Mountain, knelt down beside that huge rock thanking God for His mercy. Since then, I have consecrated that rock as my prayer rock, specifically for my brothers and sisters.

It dawned on me that Jacob had a similar experience with a rock. Of course, the stone bears no innate power of its own. Jacob in this case used the rock as a pillow and after a night of God-given dreams awoke to say, "God was here and I did not know it…. this is the gate of heaven."

I am learning that the Lord will often draw me to pray in unexpected ways for unknown reasons. I did not know when I knelt in that storm that it was the very last time I would enter the gate of heaven through prayer for my sister. I now say with Jacob, "God was in that place and I did not know it."

Your prayers matter, so keep the main thing.

—47—

Keep your word even when it costs you.
—Psalm 15:5 (MSG)

One survey says that men speak an average of 24,000 words a day and women speak about 29,000 words per day. During the election year, I wonder if we could double those stats for the candidates.

Okay, for the sake of being conservative, let's say they speak a third more words per day than the average person does. That would be 32,000 words for the male politician and 38,000 words per day for the female candidates. How many of these words are promises made to the American voter? I don't know the answer to that question, so I can't make any promises about what I'm about to write. Let's just say they make a bunch of promises.

How many of those promises do they keep? Or more to the point, how many *can* they keep to the American citizen?

Here's what I am learning. I should never make promises I don't intend to keep... or promises that would be impossible to keep even if I did intend to keep them.

And here's the tag line: Neither should politicians.

I remember the first time this chicken came home to roost in my own henhouse. I was a young pastor with far more energy than management skills, and was constantly overloading my calendar. Part of that equation was my desire to "please people" and my lack of capacity to say "no" in order to bring order to my family life, church life, and personal life.

One of my respected mentors had asked for my help and I agreed to help him on a pre-arranged date. But I had also agreed to help another person at essentially the same time. Now I know pastors like to believe they are Mr. Universe, holding up the world on their shoulders. Or maybe they visualize themselves omnipresent like God, or with the ability to fly through space and time like Phillip in Acts chapter 8.

However, it's just not true. We can't hold up the world, and we can't just say "Beam me up, Scotty" whenever we need to be transported quickly across town... or across the state. No, we can't do those things. But we can keep our word. What I did not factor into my planning was the fact that my friend and mentor was an eighty mile drive away from where I lived.

After all these years I can still see the moment in my memory and hear the Holy Spirit speak His Word to me from Psalm 15:5. I was stressed and angry -- mostly with myself -- as I drove those eighty miles.

He whispered into my heart, "Micah, I want you to learn to manage your calling well. And that requires that you honor My faithful followers and keep your promises... even when it hurts."

I got it and I am still getting it.

—48—

"I don't want your sacrifices—I want your love!
I don't want your offerings—I want you to know me!"
—Hosea 6:6 (TLB)

Hannah shivered. "It's cold in here," she said.

I looked at her and Ethan and nodded my head in agreement. We stood in one of the thousands of cathedrals sprinkled across the face of Europe. Gray stone shaped by the callused hands of craftsman long forgotten. Tall spires reached heavenward, that overshadowed bell towers and painted glass while statues stand guard for a faith now neglected. The pipe organ was quiet and the seats were empty and I was swept up into a whirlwind of spiritual history.

The murals suspended between heaven and earth, were mute and I felt the austere stare of marbled columns that had witnessed the faith of nearly a millennium of worshippers.

It was in that moment of seeming isolation that a wave of light dawned in my heart and I was suddenly filled with a holy desire to worship Creator and Father God. I had none of my usual American comforts or conveniences but worship Jesus I did. And I felt better both inside and out.

One of the most misunderstood and misused words in the human vocabulary is the word worship. It seems to me that God's loved ones in Europe and America might give similar responses to an opinion poll seeking the definition of worship.

Words like church, choir, music, mass, ritual, ceremony, and perhaps communion would be mentioned.

Standing in that cathedral I realized again that worship is not a ritual or merely a ceremony. Worship is not even music. A lot of people use the word music as a synonym for worship. Music is not worship in and of itself, especially the style of music. Worship has nothing to do with the style of music that you and I particularly like. Standing under that immense piece of architecture reminded me that worship is living a life that brings pleasure to God.

The writer of the book of Hebrews, certainly had this in mind, when he wrote, *"Make sure you don't take things for granted and go slack in working for the common good; share what you have with others. God takes particular pleasure in acts of worship—a different kind of "sacrifice"—that take place in kitchen and workplace and on the streets."* Hebrews 13:16 (MSG).

—49—

"Where is the path to the source of light?"
—*Job 38:24, (NLT)*

Long summer days are wonderful! Having grown up in the northwest, I am still surprised by the fact that it is light out until nearly 10 pm during the summer months. Light seems to make people feel better because they can get out of the house and enjoy one another and do things that, well, in the dead of winter, they can't do or just plain don't want to do.

Darkness has that kind of an effect because it is the absence of light. Light on the other hand infuses life with opportunity and joy. Father God must have had that in mind when He created light for us.

I made an interesting observation -- and it was *light* that led me to the revelation. One of the things my family and I have enjoyed doing is look for agates, which come in all shades of transparent and illustrious colors. What I have discovered is that on days when the light is diffused they are incredibly difficult to see. They blend in and hide among all the other rocks and stones. But when the light is brilliant and dazzling it refracts through the agates with laser like focus and I can see them easily. They stand out! They gleam and beam and shout, "Here I am!"

Amazing, don't you think, that a little transparency makes all the difference in the world when it comes to standing out in a crowd. Light cannot penetrate the granite, basalt or river rock, but boy, oh, boy, does it burst with dancing radiance in the transparency of an agate.

Vital and appealing physical as light may be, however, it cannot compare to the power and energy of God's spiritual light. Did you know that as a believer, you are a refractor of God's wonderful light? Multitudes of people sunbathe on sandy beaches and around back yard pools while struggling and stumbling in spiritual darkness.

A few, like Job 38:24 (NLT), query, finally weary of tripping in the dark and ask, "Where is the path to the source of light?" When they discover Jesus, like the psalmist they shout to God, "You floodlight my life!" Psalm 18:28, (MESSAGE). Still others, like the basalt rock, shut out the light. When the light flashes across their lives, it diffuses and disseminates without so much as leaving a shadow.

Sadly, they never consider what Jesus said in John 8:12 (TLB), "I am the Light of the world. So if you follow me, you won't be stumbling through the darkness, for living light will flood your path."

I heard the story told about three prospectors who hit the mother lode during the California gold rush. They sorely needed tools and supplies to mine out the treasure. They made a pact and agreed to go into town, one at a time and not utter a word to anyone. Afterward they were to meet and walk back to camp together. Only when they met to walk back to camp together, a crowd of over one hundred people had filtered out of town with them. They began to accuse one another of telling their secret, which they all denied. So they went to the crowd and asked them why they had been followed.

The spokesman for the group, simply and quickly replied, "Because we knew you had hit the big one!" "How did you know that?" the prospectors wanted to know. "Because of the beam on your faces. You could not hide your joy!"

Don't ask God to beam you up yet. Ask Him to beam you out. God is placing someone in your path right now that is looking for real light. Be transparent.

Go ahead, refract. They'll see you.

—50—

"I will cause you to become the father of a great nation. I will bless you and make you famous, and I will make you a blessing to others. I will bless those who bless you and curse those who curse you. All the families of the earth will be blessed through you."
—*Genesis 12:2-3 (NLT)*

There is an eternal blessing promised by God, to those who bless Israel. However, it is essential to underscore the meaning of the word bless. The word is illuminated with and contains the idea of benefit. In fact, *barak* (bless) is a signal from heaven that says "thank you." I like that. God says to anyone who blesses Israel, "Thank you," now receive the benefit of your blessing.

I think we must be careful not to deify Israel as we bless them. Nor should we demonize the Arab people or others who are misguided in their political and religious aims. God will deal with anyone who curses Israel, you can be certain of that.

Our purpose as believers is to pray for and bless the nation, the land and the people of Israel. I know how easy it is to be sucked into a political vacuum, which usually is sourced through the mouthpiece of the media. I would rather fall upon the promises and the Word of God.

The first time I was exposed to what is called "replacement theology" was during a return flight from Israel via Copenhagen, to Seattle. Replacement theology is as broad as it is deep, but in these few lines allow me to suffice to say that it simply means that the church has replaced Israel as God's chosen people. Consequently, all the blessings, promises and covenants God made with Israel are now the exclusive inheritance of the church. Which, by the way, led to all kinds of anti-Semitism and persecution of the Jewish people. As a result, Christians became some of the most vehement enemies and highly volatile persecutors of the Jewish people. From Martin Luther, who was energized by replacement theology and led the burning of synagogues, to the horrific practices of church officials during the Spanish Inquisition whereby so-called Jewish heretics were slowly roasted in brick ovens. This was a favorite torture called quemadero.

It is true that Jesus was clearly critical of a particular sect of the Jews called Pharisees because their belief and behavior were incongruent. Nevertheless, He said, "The teachers of religious law and the Pharisees are the official interpreters of the scriptures. So practice and obey whatever they say to you, but don't follow their example. For they don't practice what they teach" (Matthew 23:2-3, NLT).

Jesus was simply confronting what He still confronts in all of us, self-righteousness.

The New Testament unquestionably calls the church to:

- Share the gospel with Jewish people (Romans 1:16).
- Love and honor Jewish people (Ephesians 2:11-18).

And you cannot read Paul's words in Romans chapters 9-11 without imbibing his passion for his own people. *"Dear brothers and sisters, the longing of my heart and prayer to God, is that the Jewish people might be saved."* Romans 10:1 (NLT).

Then Paul announces in Romans 11:29, God's call and gifts toward Israel are without repentance. If God were not to fulfill His promises to Israel, what hope do we in the church have that He would not change His mind about His promises to you and I?

As Jeremiah 31:35-37 (NLT) points out, our God is not capricious and vacillating.

It is the LORD who provides the sun to light the day and the moon and stars to light the night. It is he who stirs the sea into roaring waves. His name is the LORD Almighty, and this is what he says: "I am as likely to reject my people Israel as I am to do away with the laws of nature! Just as the heavens cannot be measured and the foundation of the earth cannot be explored, so I will not consider casting them away forever for their sins. I, the LORD, have spoken!"

—51—

"Now it's time to change your ways! Turn to face God so he can wipe away your sins, pour out showers of blessing to refresh you, and send you the Messiah he prepared for you, namely, Jesus."
—Acts 3:19 (MSG)

I love revival...but couldn't find the word in my Bible. I love renewal, too...couldn't find that term, either. Knowing the concept was there (if not those specific words) I continued to search, excavating every variation of both words that I could think of.

Sometimes digging into God's word is more like cavernous mining than it is green grass grazing. So I moved deeper, asking the Holy Spirit for help... until I bumped my head on the stalactite of Acts 3:19, where I found the word "refresh or refreshing."

The concept is similar in meaning and expression, but much more colorful, rich, and thick with spiritual wealth. This poised me to ask some questions: What is the definition for revival that I've been carrying around in my head all these years -- and how does it line up the authentic biblical description?

Even though I have been exposed to "revival" since I was a boy, I wonder if I have really understood God's definition. For that matter, I wonder if the western church really understands that definition? What is God's purpose in sending revival? What result, fruit, or outcome is He really looking for?

As a boy, the particular church we attended insisted that revival was the time for church members to bring sinners into the building for a series of meetings, so they could be saved from their sins. Since then I have come to learn that revival is not for sinners, it is for saints. Sinners can't be revived, because they have never experienced the first "viving" -- receiving the life of God in Christ.

According to Luke's record in Acts 3:19, the cycle is something like this: repentance leads to a return to God, then comes the removal of sin, which in turn leads to a "time of refreshing" from the presence of the Lord.

I think it's important to notice the energizing source of that refreshing. What we call the day of Pentecost was not, in fact, an advertised revival meeting or conference. Nor was it a Sunday preaching series, workshop, or seminar. It was a prayer meeting.

Peter went on to inform the curious, the caustic, and the critic that the principle ingredient and criteria for refreshing, revival, and renewal was to change your mind and your ways, which we call *repentance*. Speaking of excavating words, repentance comes from the Greek term "metanoeo," which means to think differently, change your mind, or transform your mental picture and reconsider.

Like you, I ask the questions, "Change my mind about what? Think differently about who?"

I am to change my mind by thinking differently -- with a transformed thought life -- about Who Jesus really is, who I am and will become with Him, and who I am and will become without Him.

I have studied most of the great historical revivals, from the Moravians to the Charismatic renewal. Although I am a spiritual infant in this mining expedition I call revival, the concept is not new to me. In generous degrees over the past 25 years, I have experienced revival and renewal from the Holy Spirit.

Each day for one week, my wife and I stood in long lines from early morning to evening in front of the Brownsville Assembly of God in Florida. We would take our lawn chairs, ice chest and umbrellas and sit until the doors opened, so we could join the throng in rushing inside to find a good seat for the evening gathering.

Now that I think back on that experience, I wonder if we really understood God's heart. The main ingredient in revival is not the place or even the people; *it is the presence of God that is invaluable and irreplaceable for revival, renewal, and refreshing.* Even faithful disciples need to be refreshed in God's presence and renew their covenant call. Paul had to remind Pastor Timothy to "fan into flame the gift of God, which is in you through the laying on of my hands" (1 Timothy 1:6, NIV).

My purpose is not to critique any revival or to present a biblical theology of revival. I'm simply asking the questions, what should be the result of revival? What is the evident kingdom fruit? Why does God send what we today call revival? What does He require of His people when they are revived? What does He ask us to do as revived people?

So whether you prefer renewal, revival or refreshing as the call sign of heaven's outpouring, as God's child, if you have it, what are you doing with it? If you get it, where will you take it?

An old Alabama preacher said it well and clear many years ago, "The Lord ain't so concerned with how high ya jump, as He is with how far ya run with Jesus when ya hit the ground."

—52—

All of this happened to fulfill the Lord's message through his prophet:
"Look! The virgin will conceive a child! She will give birth to a son,
and He will be called Immanuel, (meaning, God is with us)."
—Matthew 1:22-23 (NLT)

Years ago a man I respect told me, "Reality is not what you think, it is what you *do*." Obviously, the point is well made and remains true. What I feel and what I think are always suspect. The reservoir of my own soul is not a reliable indicator of God's ultimate truth or a clear picture of His full plan. What we think or feel is happening is not always accurate. Nor can we fully see the big picture from the frame of reference offered by our thoughts and feelings.

Mary no doubt believed that she was experiencing labor pains because she was about to deliver a baby, indeed a very special baby according to Gabriel's stunning words (Luke 1). *What Mary didn't know in her moment of pain is that she was birthing the Savior of the whole world.*

Pretty staggering stuff if you ask me. Mary conceived from God and produced a miracle. However, having never experienced physical labor or birth pangs, I can only rely on the seven times I have walked that out with my dear wife, Nancy, as she clutched my shirt saying, "What have you done to me!"

Having experienced those moments with Nancy, I highly doubt Mary thought about the Messiah, who thirty three years later would be falsely accused, beaten, crucified, died and risen from the dead three days later. Mary gave birth to a baby whom she would readily love, nurture and joyfully care for.

That was her reality for the moment. I don't know what you are conceiving right now, but I do know that if you and I conceive anything from Father God it will be good. Usually we forget that pain settles in on the heels of conception and then birth gives way to deliverance and relief.

How easy it is to go through each day merely looking at things, people and even God, but never really seeing. When I was a boy, I remember seeing a painting of Daniel in the lion's den. Back then, I didn't see the most significant aspect of that painting. That Daniel didn't have his eyes on the lions, he had his eyes on the Lord.

—53—

Uzziah sought God during the days of Zechariah,
who instructed him in the fear of God. And as long
as he sought the LORD, God gave him success.
—2 Chronicles 26:5 (NLT)

Believe me, I know very well how easy it is to be distracted and end up tripping-- and even falling flat. The good news is we can recover by seeking God with a humble heart.

It's not surprising that the Hebrew word for "sought" means *to follow* and more specifically *to worship God.* And herein lies the key to real, lasting success.

"Success," of course, can mean different things to different people. It's clear however, that Father God is keenly interested in the success of His children. He loves to watch us fly down the trail He has prepared for us. Does that mean our way will be easy? Not at all. But will it be worth it? Absolutely, if you pay attention to your course, your footing, and your guide, the Holy Spirit.

Digging deeper into King Uzziah's life you will discover that his success and influence were profound, as recorded in 2 Chronicles 26:7-15. However, there is a sad footnote to Uzziah's story. In 2 Chronicles 26:16 (NLT) we read: "But when he had become powerful, he also became proud, which led to his downfall."

The Message translation puts it in blunt terms: "Everything seemed to go his way. But then the strength and success went to his head. Arrogant and proud, he fell... contemptuous of God."

What happened? Better yet, what *changed?* Uzziah ceased worshipping the Lord and begin to believe his own press.

Winston Churchill correctly noted, "Success is not final and failure is not fatal."

King Uzziah was a successful man with loyal troops and closely aligned friends with all the marvelous perks a man could hope or wish for. I believe the use of old, Elizabethan English is necessary to make my point.

He forgot the pit from which he was dug, and the rock from which he was hewn.

Here are Paul's words to the Galatians church: "You were running the race so well. Who has held you back from following the truth?" (Galatians 5:7, NLT).

It was true of Uzziah and true of the Galatians. It is also true of you and me. If you reach any pinnacle of success, watch out.

Self is a tyrant king.

—54—

"Using a dull ax requires great strength, so sharpen the blade.
That's the value of wisdom; it helps you succeed."
—*Ecclesiastes 10:10 (NLT)*

Who was it that said, "Repetition is the mother of skill?" In other words, if you practice something consistently at some task, you'll become better at it.

There is insight to be garnered from that truism. Simply stated, skill is shaped by forming good habits. Discipline is not readily embraced by most, but it can save your job and perhaps your life.

Let me illustrate:

There was a young man who went to a logging foreman seeking a job as a tree faller. The foreman told him, "I have a full crew, and I don't need any help." The young man said, "I can outwork your entire crew. I will fall more trees than all of your men combined." The foreman was impressed with his confidence. So he offered him a one-week job on a trial basis. "If you are able to do what you claim for one week, I'll give you the job." The young man agreed.

Sure enough, after the first day he had fallen more trees than the entire crew combined. And, also, on the second and third day. On the forth day the foreman noticed that although he was still working just as hard, he fell behind the crew. The trend continued on the fifth, sixth, and seventh days. At the end of the seventh day the foreman met with the very tired young man.

"I don't understand it," the young man said wearily. "I worked just as hard today as I did the first day and yet I only cut a third of the trees."

The foreman looked at him and said, "You've learned a valuable lesson."

"Yeah, I'd like to know what that is," he responded.

With years of experience the seasoned old logger replied, *"You forgot to sharpen your ax!"*

Go ahead, take a break and sharpen your ax.

—55—

The LORD is my shepherd; I have all that I need.
—Psalm 23:1 (NLT)

Springtime in Israel is extraordinary. Even extraordinary cannot sufficiently describe how stunning the wild flowers are as they dance in their splendor across the green hillsides.

I stood on top of a hill in Israel near the town of Zorah. You know the one I refer to, don't you? Zorah is where Samson grew up. More specifically, I was standing on the hilltop that once carried the ancient town of Bet Shemesh. The history of Bet Shemesh, which means "house of the sun," tells us that this is the place where King David began the process of returning the Ark of the Covenant to the holy city of Jerusalem.

As I stood there looking across the valley of Zoreq, taking in this scene, a shepherd walked up the hill toward us with more than two hundred sheep following him. A small boy walked beside the flock, towards the back.

Immediately, I was riveted to this picture, with such deep and ancient roots. The flock moved almost fluid like across the new green grass. I noticed that the shepherd stayed in front of sheep and with no more than the sound of his voice and a wave of his arm the flock would change direction. It was an incredible sight to watch. I was riveted by the corporate harmony below me not more than one hundred yards distant.

There is something else to take note of from this experience. At any given time, there were ten to twenty of the sheep leaping, almost bucking, as they twisted in the air, leaping and darting out of the flow of the flock, as if to chart their own course. Another ten percent appeared to be in some kind of confrontation as they switched direction and faced against the flow of the flock and butted heads and pushed other smaller sheep around if possible.

Do you know what really fascinated me? The shepherd never ran into the flock attempting to separate the combatants. Neither did he rush back to cut the runaways off as they flitted this way and that, challenging the direction of the flock. Occasionally, the shepherd's small assistant would correct a wayward sheep, but the shepherd remained out front doing what shepherds do; leading and feeding the sheep. He kept moving and never seemed to be dismayed or angered, even though there were moments it seemed the flock would break into factions and smaller bands of rogue units. Even the goats blending in the flock didn't detour the shepherds mission. I was mesmerized by this phenomenon.

The shepherd did not drive the sheep, he led them.

Truly this is a marvelous lesson of the shepherd in action.

—56—

If you wait for perfect conditions, you will never get anything done.
—Ecclesiastes 11:4, (NLT)

I slowly creaked and crackled out of bed, feeling more like a wooden man than anything remotely organic. My whole body hurt from a symphony of sore muscles. Lactic acid terrorized all major muscle groups like a gang of anarchists, vandalized and burned its way through quads and calves. My joints seemed welded together, as I grimaced my way to an upright position. For the past week, I had been training hard, and now the battle lines were drawn.

I have learned from twenty years of trail running that rest days are essential. I have also learned that sore muscles are an encouragement to stick with it and not give up because something always seems to hurt. In fact, a little more exercise will help *heal* sore muscles.

And it is here, at this point, with the first signs of soreness, where so many people become intimidated and raise the white flag of surrender, never reaching their full potential. Believe me, I understand the challenge. It isn't easy carving out the time to exercise in the midst of a busy schedule, creating a balanced discipline, setting goals, or rolling a protesting body out of bed in the early morning to put on my running gear. I have to grit my teeth sometimes, just like you do. There are days when it is very, very difficult to stay the course and hold the line.

Training hurts. As I groaned through my stretches, fighting my way back to something more limber and loose, my mind swept back over my long experience on the trail.

Any physiologist worth their salt will tell you that some degree of muscle soreness is to be expected, especially in the beginning of your workout program. Don't let that throw you. And don't quit! Hang in there, and push through the pain as long as it's not a chronic injury. The fact is, your muscles are adapting to your discipline and will not fall into formation without resistance.

Every spring you see people get excited about working out, losing those unneeded pounds, and getting into shape. Then after the first couple of workouts and the first assault of the muscle anarchists, they're shocked by how sore they feel. *Really* sore.

They're not accustomed to it. They don't like it, and many give up and quit, while telling themselves, "I'll do it someday," weighing in on the calendar, focusing only on future tense for the more perfect conditions and missing the here and now.

Someday...

—57—

*God wants us to grow up, to know the whole truth and
tell it in love—like Christ in everything. We take our lead
from Christ, who is the source of everything we do.*
—Ephesians 4:15 (MSG)

Two pastors from local churches were standing by the side of the road pounding a sign into the ground that read: *"The end is near! Turn yourself around now, before it's too late!"*

"Leave us alone you religious nuts!" yelled a driver as he sped by. From around the curve the pastors heard screeching tires and a big splash.

One pastor turned to the other and asked, "Do you think the sign should just say 'Bridge Out'?"

For a long time I carried a piece of paper in my wallet that said, "It is never as bad as you think it is." Over the years I have found that to be true. On the other hand, when going through a tough time the first thoughts attempting deep impact my brain are usually dark messages like, "This is terrible, and it can't get any worse than this!" O yes, it can get worse and it will!

It is true, 95% of the things we humans worry about never happen. If the opposite of love is fear, then perhaps I would do well to see the opposite of faith is worry. Worry is negative faith. Look at it this way. If you have the emotional energy and spiritual strength to worry that something bad is coming true, then you have the emotional energy and spiritual strength to have faith in God for good things. The kind and caliber of faith that confronts those fears and worries in the power of Christ.

In the crucible of crisis, Paul reminds us from a prison cell,

"Don't fret or worry. Instead of worrying, pray. Let petitions and praises shape your worries into prayers, letting God know your concerns. Before you know it, a sense of God's wholeness, everything coming together for good, will come and settle you down. It's wonderful what happens when Christ displaces worry at the center of your life." Philippians 4:6-7 (MSG)

Is the end near? I don't know if it is near or not. But I do know that listening to voices cloaked as truth and vacant of love lead to a vacuum of hopelessness.

Perhaps I should just say, "Bridge out ahead!"

—58—

"You shall remember that the L<small>ORD</small> *your God led you all the way these forty years in the wilderness...."*
—Deuteronomy 8:2, (NKJV)

This is a difficult message to write; deeply personal and profoundly painful as I probe its dimensions.

The story begins when I met my wife to be, Nancy. I soon discovered what great people her parents were. Her dad laughed a lot, he was generous and kind and the tenth and youngest child of first generation German emigrants.

Nancy's mother was a corporate secretary, sharp, intelligent and known far and wide for her keen ability to remember hundreds of people's names. I heard that story repeated many times, as someone would tell me how Nancy's mother met them one time, the next time they would walk into the office and she would call them by their first name.

Alzheimer's struck her hard and fast at age 49, robbing her of any vestiges of memory or recall. It was so very sad. Nancy's dad did his best to care for her. Slowly, friends stopped coming by and they stopped going out in public.

It was on Father's Day, 1984, we were at our first pastorate in Olympia, Washington, preparing to go to the evening worship with our small children.

The phone rang and it was one of Nancy's brothers bearing almost unbelievable news. He had come by the folk's house to wish his dad a happy Father's Day.

149

As he entered the house, he found Nancy's mother seated in a living room chair, staring blankly at the television. He called to his dad but no answer came. As he made his way down the hallway, the first door on the left was the family bathroom. There on the floor lay his dad's body. We soon learned that Nancy's dad had died from a heart attack. Charles Quast was fifty six years old.

That entire day Nancy's mom sat in her chair oblivious to what was lost. We made preparations and quickly traveled to be with Nancy's two brothers.

After the memorial services, Nancy and her two older brothers were faced with how to care for their mother. She had deteriorated so rapidly that she required full time care and attention.

Finding an Alzheimer care facility was very difficult because they were unheard of in those days. They finally found a facility willing to take her, so I volunteered to help Nancy's brothers take her there the first time.

I shall never forget that day. It is branded upon my soul, for as we sat her on the bed, having done all we could in that moment to make sure she had what she needed, we turned to leave, I heard her say, "Wally, Kenny, Nancy!"

That's all she said and at first it was slow and quiet and as we continued to walk away, her voice became louder and more shrill, "Wally, Kenny, Nancy!" Then again with machine gun rapidity, "Wally, Kenny, Nancy!" She called out loudly to the point that Nancy's brother was overcome with emotion.

The only three words that she was crying out were the three names of her children. For perhaps a year, Nancy's mother had not been able to have any kind of intelligible conversation.

But in that moment of desperation, feeling the reality of utter separation, something in her consciousness compelled her to leap across the gulf of nothingness, feeling her way along dark cerebral corridors, until she saw some glimmer of light.

And all she could utter was what had been most dear to her heart, "Wally, Kenny and Nancy!"

When the Holy Spirit brought this memory to the forefront of my mind, I initially pushed it back into my own system of filing things, pressing it down as something I would rather not think about. A rabbi's old story says it clearly.

The first generation knew how to build the altar, where to gather the wood, how to build the fire, prepare the sacrifice and worship. The next generation knew how to build the altar, where to gather the wood, how to build the fire, prepare the sacrifice. The third generation knew how to build the altar, where to gather the wood, how to build the fire. The next knew how to build the altar and where to gather the wood. Finally, no one knew how to build an altar.

—59—

"Let not your hearts faint, fear not, and do not tremble...."
—Deuteronomy 20:3, (KJV)

Years ago, I experienced a frightening phenomenon that literally made my hair stand up. While running alone along a barren ridge late one afternoon, I could see the sweeping farmland, dropping away to the south, into the Columbia River trough, splitting the boundaries between the states of Oregon and Washington. To the north, rising out of the desert, was the mammoth spine of Rattlesnake Mountain.

It was a euphoric moment. People out west say that if you don't like the weather in the springtime, wait ten minutes and it will change. Well, that's true. When I began moving up the ridge, the sky was a deep blue and the sun was shining. But now, huge, black clouds were gathered overhead. They seemed to bulge and pulsate as if some living creature was inside trying to fight and push its way out.

Then it happened. At first I was surprised when I noticed that my hair was standing on end. You know what I mean, it was static and vibrating, as if magnetized. Then it dawned on me, I was forming up to serve as a ground for lightning to rise off the terra firma into the thunderhead above me. That is when the alarm bells went off.

I quickly assessed the situation formulating my options... and then took off running as fast as my two hundred pounds could move. After running a hundred yards up the ridge and eating both of my socks, I confessed that even if I could run like Robert or George, I couldn't outrun lightening.

There was not even a hint of anything around to protect me. So I stopped, raised both hands and said, "Lord, as always I am in Your hands." I calmed down a bit and continued to jog along the ridge and finally down the trail back to my pickup.

I later talked to one of my friends who understood the conduction of electricity better than I and he confirmed my worst case fear scenario.

Something electrifying and more powerful than I passed by me.

Did you know a guy named Eliphaz, in the book of Job, shared a similar experience? However, it was supernatural in origin. He said, "A spirit glided right in front of me, the hair on my head stood on end" Job 4:15 (Message).

I can identify with that feeling. The fact of the matter is, everyday you and I are shadowed by forces, both natural and supernatural more powerful than we are. God speaks through such methods and means. The psalmist said of Creator God, "The winds are your messengers; flames of fire are your servants" (Psalm 104:4, NLT). Even the men we call "the disciples" experienced God speaking in the fierce winds of a storm. At first, they misinterpreted the message, even more importantly, they did not recognize Jesus in the tumultuous blast. When they "saw him, they screamed in terror, thinking He was a ghost."

There are layers, dimensions and degrees of natural and supernatural storms blowing over us these days. Even if they cause the hair on your head to stand straight up, recognize who Jesus is and hear His voice speak to you in the tempest, "It's all right. I am here! Don't be afraid."

—60—

Don't grieve God. Don't break His heart. His Holy Spirit, moving
and breathing in you, is the most intimate part of your life,
making you fit for Himself. Don't take such a gift for granted.
—Ephesians 4:30 (MSG)

When I stood with my cousin, Jon Smith, and friend, Dicky Hartman, on the edge of Mill Creek in central Oklahoma, I saw a very unusual sight. The creek generally runs north and south as it cuts its quiet way through the hills. The tree-lined banks served as sentries where occasional splashes of white cascaded from the blossoms of the dogwood tree that clashed with the deep hued glow of the red bud.

I saw and heard the shrill whistle of the red cardinal and the mimicking cry of the mocking bird. In the distance, there was the lonely but persistent call of a turkey. It was one of those days that I wish I could bottle up and savor for a long time.

All my senses were moving in sync, and I knew this is what it felt like to be fully alive. I know you are wondering what was so unusual about my experiences. Just this. At one point the creek took a drop that probably maxed out at twenty to twenty five feet. As the water began its rapid decent, it was met with the strong backhand of a huge and solid rock formation.

What I saw in this boiling, surging and threatening torrent was two ninety-degree turns within thirty feet of each other and all in solid rock. When the water hit the first ninety-degree turn it was met with such a backlash that it created an eddy of

155

backwater that moved in and out as if it was an ocean tide. It was a truly remarkable sight. With persistence, the water sought out a quick recourse and continued to flow over a fall and down into the next ninety-degree turn flushed out under intense hydraulic pressure, which tumbled, turned and sprayed its way into a once again calm and steady force.

I told my cousin that it reminded me of something the Holy Spirit had spoken to my heart two years previously. While flying over the eastern seaboard, I noticed something that had often intrigued me; the unbelievable switchbacks as a river twisted and turned its course below. As I observed this earthly canvas of revelation, I asked the Holy Spirit, "Why doesn't the river flow straight?" Without hesitation He responded, "Because rivers take the route of least resistance." Immediately I understood. Any hardness repels the water to flow another direction.

More importantly, any hardness of heart I may hold on to simply causes Him to flow another direction. Any resistance to His move, any opposition to His flow, any challenge to His Lordship, any refusal to accept His guidance or correction or love is like that creek, even to the point of taking two hard ninety-degree turns on the path of least resistance. He moves where He is welcome.

No doubt Paul had that in mind when he wrote, "Do not stifle the Holy Spirit" (1 Thessalonians 5:19, NLT). The idea is … don't suppress the Holy Spirit in any way. I must move with Him, not against Him. I wonder if Paul was looking at a river when he wrote those words?

Now back to those dogwoods…

—61—

My dear brothers and sisters, be quick to listen,
slow to speak, and slow to get angry.
—*James 1:19 (NLT)*

A friend goaded me into thinking about the art of communication the other day when he inquired as to whether I was taciturn or not. This little used word simply means, "Disinclined to talk." Given the antonym Loquacious, which means "full of excessive talk," I would have to say, yes, I am.

There is any number of reasons for my monosyllabic mindset, not the least having been on more than one occasion, the willing victim of, "Open mouth, and insert foot."

Like the time I asked a dear lady if she was pregnant. No, she was not! Or the intense embarrassment I felt when I requested that a fellow introduce me to his mother. She was his wife. In the words of Lewis Sperry Chafer, "It's much better to keep silent and let everybody think you're a fool, than to open your mouth and remove all doubt."

Which reminds me of my early mentoring on the subject with the admonition of Martin Luther's theology on sermonizing: "Stand up, Speak up and Shut up." Or just say what you mean and mean what you say.

I am not defending the strong silent type who isn't necessarily strong just silent. Please don't stone me. I am simply re-visiting a value that has been sacrificed in our wordy information, saturated age.

Charles Jehlinger, at one time, filled the position of the director of the American Academy of Dramatic Arts. He frequently instructed his apprentice actors with five words of advice: "Mean more than you say."

We followers of Jesus could benefit from that counsel. In the succinct words of another, "we feel compelled to analyze, philosophize, scrutinize and moralize" with endless waves of verbiage, (Sigh), (hum), until we are all weary and bored, (Yawn). There is far too much gobbledygook in the world today.

Let's start a revolution, one that follows the genius of Jesus' communication style. He simplified and clarified issues that religionists confused and complicated.

Children loved Him for it!

Like the Wall Street Journal put it: "When's the best time to stop talking?" Probably now.

—62—

But Christ has rescued us from the curse pronounced
by the law. When he was hung on the cross, he took
upon himself the curse for our wrongdoing.
—Galatians 3:13 (NLT)

I stood beside a casket of a friend who left us much too early. I had journeyed with Paul and Tammy Wulff for a few years, as she battled an aggressive brain tumor. At the same time, Paul was a highly successful football coach for Eastern State University in Cheney, Washington. Many prayers had gone before Father God for Tammy, but He chose to take her to be with Him, rather than leave her with us.

When Paul contacted me about officiating his wife's memorial service, I accepted. Family, friends, college and NFL coaches and players made their way to Tammy's childhood parish in Seattle, Washington. The place was packed as I shared from John 11 and Jesus' promise to His followers, of resurrection and life.

Tammy Wulff lived on this earth for a mere thirty-nine years, yet my heart was comforted by the profound sense of God's love and presence. *It was sad but not despairing.*

May I be vulnerable for a moment? These kinds of experiences compel me to revisit the foot of the cross. Without the experience of Jesus' horrific suffering on the cross, there would be no story, hope or promise of the resurrection.

Please don't misunderstand. Jesus is alive and resurrection life and power are available and unquenchable. You see, it is not possible to think about the cross very long, before my perspective is adjusted and my purpose is again clarified. Every believer benefits from such a journey as this; especially those who lead and influence others for Jesus.

In his letter to the Corinthians, the apostle Paul expresses his heart on the cross of Christ: "God did not send me to collect a following for myself, but to preach the message of what He has done, collecting a following for Him. And He didn't send me to do it with a lot of fancy rhetoric of my own, lest the powerful action at the center.... Christ on the cross... be trivialized into mere words. The message that points to Christ on the cross seems like sheer silliness to those hell-bent on destruction, but for those on the way to salvation it makes perfect sense" 1 Corinthians 1:17-18 (MSG).

Selfishness and a my-way attitude loses altitude at the foot of the cross. Smallness of soul and a hyper introspection somehow dissipates into His light or withdraws back into the shadows when I see Jesus lifted up on the cross.

The church needs the cross.

George MacLeod says it better than I.

> I simply argue that the cross be raised again
> at the center of the market place
> as well as on the steeple of the church,
> I am recovering the claim that
> Jesus was not crucified in a cathedral
> between two candles:
> But on a cross between two thieves;
> on a town garbage heap;
> at a crossroad of politics so cosmopolitan
> that they had to write His title
> in Hebrew and in Latin and in Greek...
> And at the kind of place where cynics talk smut,

and thieves curse and soldiers gamble.
Because that is where He died,
and that is what He died about.
And that is where Christ's men ought to be,
and what church people ought to be about.

So, once again, in the fervor of social sickness, political fallout, religious wars, and personal sadness, I go back to the cross. And again it all makes sense.

—63—

"(God) is not far from any one of us.
For in Him we live and move and exist."
—Acts 17:27-28 (NLT)

Have you ever considered the possibility that there may be one thing in your life you are not willing to release or do or even budge on, even if God specifically were to ask you to do so? Little by little, Jesus has been teaching me about that one thing in my own heart. My steps on that pathway have been numerous and I am by no means there yet, but I am pressing on.

In 2000, we heard the Holy Spirit's call to return with my wife and children to the area where I grew up. It has been no secret that I did not want to "come home" and it was not some premeditated sense of rebellion or hard heartedness that I was experiencing. *Rather, it was my perception.*

It wasn't that I had zero good memories growing up, but that some of the bad memories seemed so enormous that there was hardly room for me to see anything else through the window of the past. There was a lot of pain to face on many levels.

That is not to say that all of those bad memories can be laid at the feet of someone else; some of the responsibility lies at my feet because there comes a time in a person's life when they can no longer blame what someone else did for their choices; some of my painful past was due to my decisions, no one else's.

Yet, Father God does not pull off His rescue plan as we would think and in His mysterious ways He called us to move back home and live.

The good news is that Jesus healed me. Don't think for a moment that this happened the first week we moved back home to live. It didn't and it took time because inside I was kicking, screaming and dragging my feet.

I'm thinking about a two-frame cartoon I read recently. There are two people in each frame, Jesus (smiling) and another person. First frame, Jesus says, "My child, I never left you. Those places with one set of foot prints, it was then that I carried you. Second frame, Jesus points over to the side and says, "That long groove over there. That was when I dragged you for a while." *Hmmm, that sounds a bit too much like me...*

Where once I may have driven down a certain street or saw a certain person and my senses of sight and sound and sometimes smell triggered a wave of sadness or anger, as the memory, like a sea creature that rose up from the murky depths of my soul taunted me to live with it once again. Father God in mercy has set me free from those past haunting perceptions.

The wise words of Proverbs frames it all, "How can we understand the road we travel? It is the LORD who directs our steps" Proverbs 20:24 (NLT).

Here's what I've learned.

It is not God's will for one of His kids to live with a gun from the past held to their heads as a hostage to pain.

When Jesus asks you to run with Him, just do it.

And try not to leave such a big groove.

—64—

*From there (Jesus) went all over Galilee. He used synagogues
for meeting places and taught people the truth of God. God's
kingdom was his theme, that beginning right now they were
under God's government, a good government! He also healed
people of their diseases and of the bad effects of their bad lives.*
—Matthew 4:23 (MSG)

Daybreak this morning, I woke up to an old familiar
sound... the wind. Our house shuddered and creaked,
straining against its unrelenting press, push, and heave.
As I gazed under the window blind, I could see the evidence
of the sounds reaching my ears. Trees were bent this way, then
that, bushes shook by an unseen hand. Not audibly, but in my
heart, I heard the Holy Spirit's reminder of the words of Jesus,
"The wind blows where it wishes, and you hear the sound of
it, but cannot tell where it comes from and where it goes. So is
everyone who is born of the Spirit" (John 3:8 NKJV). *I felt safe.*

Jesus didn't mince words when He told a real religious guy,
"Unless a person is born from above, it's not possible to see what
I'm pointing to -- to God's kingdom" John 3:3, (MESSAGE).

I understand why people do not necessarily knock down the
doors to church buildings, just because Christians say things
like that. Why should anyone want to see God's kingdom? It
is a valid and good question, requiring a thoughtful response.

It seems to me that man's quest has been, well, from the beginning, a longing for three things; The Bible calls it righteousness, or being right, and living right.

In other words, we humans articulate as "Am I ok?"

God did not leave us hanging out on a broken limb here. He makes the connection between "seeing" which interestingly enough, the Greek word "Ido" found in Strong's Concordance at number 1492, sounds like a new world discovery to me. It is not merely seeing, the word "Ido" also means, "knowing."

You can know you are okay, because of peace, which is a sense of well-being and an absence of anxiety. And joy, the ability to sing with all your heart, without accompaniment, being "born again or born from above." Jesus also said, "Don't be so surprised when I tell you that you have to be 'born from above,' out of this world, so to speak. You know well enough how the wind blows this way and that. You hear it rustling through the trees, but you have no idea where it comes from or where it's headed next. That's the way it is with everyone 'born from above' by the wind of God, the Spirit of God" John 3:7-8, (MESSAGE).

One philosopher said, "Not everything that is faced can be changed, but nothing can be changed until it is faced."

What you see is what you know. What direction are you looking? You may need to turn and face the wind.

—65—

I have trailblazed a preaching of the Message of Jesus all the
way from Jerusalem far into northwestern Greece. This has
all been pioneer work, bringing the Message only into those
places where Jesus was not yet known and worshiped.
—Romans 15:19-20 (MSG)

Winter is a sore loser. Through the past month this sassy season has whined every time spring has slapped his frigid fingers. He has whipped snow with tempestuous gusts and growled threats, but little by little, spring is prying loose his icy grip, and life is bursting forth. *Life always wins out in the end.*

As winter sulks away and springtime leaps with joy, so do I. This season of transition has given me an occasional opportunity to build a walking, running, and praying trail behind my house. The loop is about a mile in length, and covers a bench of land held above the river by massive basalt cliffs. What I have done -- with the help of my wife and son -- is connect a few ancient game trails by clearing brush, moving some rocks, and being adventuresome.

Brilliant yellow buttercups carpet places along the trail, cared for by a Master Gardener. Bald eagles and red-tailed hawks soar overhead, while elk and deer sneak through stands of Douglas fir, tamarack, and pine. Flocks of wild turkey along the trail practice for their annual mating dance. Throw in bluebirds, nuthatches, goldfinches, chickadees, pheasants, doves, and woodpeckers, and well… the woods are a lively, lovely place in the springtime.

Trailblazing is exhilarating, and dangerous. Our neighbors have seen bears, mountain lions, and wolves in this same area. As we cut our way through some of the overgrown places of the trail, I thought of friends and family who, in their own right, are trailblazers and pioneers. People who are not afraid to take a risk, daring to move into the future God has forged for them. People who think outside the proverbial box and refuse to take the safe route, the easy route, or the quick and popular route. People who make it happen day in and day out, and most of the world doesn't even know their names.

But God does. And ultimately, what else matters?

These men and women are like Jesus… courageous, generous, giving, and loving. They squeeze every drop out of every season of life they enter into. They serve, pray, and trust when there is no reason -- or at least, visible reason -- to do so. Like the buttercup that finally breaks through winter's grip, they know that God is their source, Jesus is their master, and the Holy Spirit is their guide. So they press on, carving the path before them with joy and sometimes tears.

I think of you pioneers -- breaking trails, moving rocks, uprooting obstacles, keeping a wary eye for mountain lions, and running with perseverance the race set before you -- and bow my head with gratitude. Nancy and I thank God for the treasure of your lives, and the trails you have built, so others can follow.

—66—

You have not handed me over to my enemies
but have set me in a safe place.
—Psalm 31:8 (NLT)

Water dripped from the chiseled basalt ceiling -- some places in a steady stream -- or seeped down the black rock walls. Deeper inside, icicles dangled, suspended like an inverted pipe organ. The passageway was dark, dank, and odious. *And I wanted out.*

With my dog, Eli Sackett, at my side, we had entered the Canadian Pacific train tunnel, quickly lost all sense of the warm sunlight outside. I saw where a deer had been hit, never suspecting its horrific danger in that passageway. I shivered and I kept moving.

The tracks were lonely and isolated from any traces of urban life. At the same time, weaved as they do along the sheer basalt cliffs high above the Kootenai River, they have a mystery and beauty about them as well. There were spots where the tracks cut across the shoulder of the bluff, which dropped away with a dizzying effect. At times Eli and I would stop and peer over the edge, look down at the blue-green water of the Kootenai as it swirled in pools and eddies, and moved toward British Columbia.

Our route took us through several tunnels, cut through solid basalt rock. Before I entered a tunnel I stopped and listened for any sign or sound of a train coming around the bend. For extra measure, I knelt down and placed my hand on the track, because trains will send a vibration along the steel arteries upon which they live.

Since the Holy Spirit has never spoken to me in a train tunnel before, I was a little surprised when He said, *"I am going to teach you about tunnel vision."*

Tunnel vision isn't something that's uppermost in my mind as I negotiate a dark train tunnel. My mission is always singular: get through that thing *fast.* My one consuming desire is that proverbial "light at the end of the tunnel," cast its rays of freedom down the shaft, that reflect off the steel tracks.

"Okay, Lord," I responded, not slowing my pace. "I'm listening."

He continued, *"I am alerting you to avoid tunnel vision."* The Holy Spirit had my full attention as Eli and I emerged from the tunnel's mouth and continued our trek down the tracks.

Medically speaking, of course, I know that tunnel vision is a loss of peripheral sight and the ability to see outside the center of one's gaze. Unexpectedly in that moment the Holy Spirit spoke to me about tunnel vision in *life* and showed me how personal pain can cause any one of us to lose our full range of sight. I've been there at times, and I bet you have, too. We can become so transfixed on our pain that it's all we see, blinding us to any other person or aspect of life and reality. Pain and all of its manifestations become -- for a time, at least -- our reality.

But then we come out of the tunnel into the light. Or at least… we should. Sometimes, however, people don't emerge from the place of perpetual night. Pain becomes the center of their universe, the gravity that holds their vision captive. Growing anxiety and a refusal to take personal responsibility for one's actions reduce light to a narrow beam, where freedom and spacious living become impossible. Pain narrows one's view of God and people, icing up the heart. An individual gripped by pain becomes overwhelmed and controlled by a victim mentality.... the blame game. "My pain is someone else's fault," they claim.

They may well be right. They may have a good case to make, but "being right" doesn't get you out of the dark tunnel. "Being right" will never release you from the black and narrow confines of grief, grudges, and guilt.

God's mission is to get us *through* the tunnel, to move us past our pain and back into the warm sunlight of happier days.

I considered where I might be afflicted with tunnel vision in my own life, and made up my mind to get through all such deep, dark passageways -- and back out into the light and fresh air. With God helping me, I don't want to be overcome by forces that drive people in a direction and toward a destination they never planned to arrive at in their lives.

As the Chinese proverb says, "a journey of a thousand miles begins with the first step."

In other words, *direction determines destination.* I thought about that as Eli Sackett and I left the tracks and struck out on a narrow trail that angled up the hill and back to level ground.

—67—

Don't lose your grip on Love and Loyalty. Tie them around
your neck; carve their initials on your heart. Earn a reputation
for living well in God's eyes and the eyes of the people...
Love and truth form a good leader; sound
leadership is founded on loving integrity.
—Proverbs 3:3, 20:28 (MSG)

I looked at my watch and groaned inside. Our journey from India, thus far, had taken 16 hours -- and our flight from Munich to Frankfurt was still one hour out. The last leg was an 11-hour flight back to Seattle. India was a long way from home.

I scanned the early morning commuters gathered at the gate inside the Munich terminal, mostly German businessmen and women, neatly dressed and manicured, some read the newspaper, others chatted on mobile phones, all looked sharp and ready for the day's challenges.

My mind wandered back a few days to the creak of carts, horns beeping amid a flurry of bicycles and taxis which bantered for position on a busy, over-crowded street in India. To my western mind there seemed to be no rhyme or reason as to how these people managed to move through the city center of Udaipur, in the Indian state of Rajasthan. Women moved with seamless fluidity and carried large pots on their heads, their saris flowed in the hot breeze. Cattle wandered through the bustle of traffic and locals without concern, sometimes they stopped in the middle of the street to lie down or simply nap while they stood up.

Small shops lined both sides of the busy street, where shop owners busied themselves with eking out another day of sustenance. I saw metal workers who squatted as they tapped pieces of metal, bending and shaping them to their will. Fruit vendors held ancient looking scales in one hand, added small counterweights with the other, and balanced the fruit being purchased by a prospective customer. All the while, they volleyed words back and forth, as the deal was made.

The dark face of my young guide was expressionless when I casted a glance his way. Awan, I had discovered over several days of working together, was both shy and sincere. More than a guide, he had also served as my translator during teaching sessions and ceremonies. When I had pressed him to take me to a nearby 4000-foot Bansdara Mountain, he did not quite understand what I wanted to do. Finally, after talking for several minutes, he understood that I wanted to run from the bottom of the mountain to the top.

"Do you have medical insurance?" He wanted to know, shaking his head from side to side.

"Yes, I do," I replied. "Why do you ask?"

"Because it is very hot," he said, almost casually, "and you may need it."

This young man impressed me.

Having come from the state of Orissa in India, he was well acquainted with persecution and suffering for his faith in Christ. More than three thousand of the thirty-six thousand people estimated to be homeless because of the barbaric, hostility aimed at Christians, came from his church fellowship. He knew of two pastors who had been killed, multiple church buildings burned down, and families chased from their generational homes, property, and communities.

We walked into one of the shops where my wife purchased some inexpensive earrings. Earlier, I had asked Awan about his family. He was married, he'd told me, but his wife was back in Orissa and lived with his dad and mom. He hoped to see her before Easter. I felt prompted to buy a pair of earrings for Awan to give his wife as a gift. After I urged him, he picked out a pair and we walked back out into the hustle and bustle of the city street. As we had walked, he handed the earrings back to me. We stopped on the street and I looked into his eyes, prepared to protest.

"My mentor and I have always been very transparent with each other. I have always done as he asked of me with joy. I have never received any money or gifts for doing this. Before I can accept them, I would want him to know."

"Nothing material must ever come between us or harm our relationship."

My protest dissolved as my admiration for this young kingdom leader went up. I have never encountered such loyal integrity. It both inspired me and convicted me.

The loudspeaker jolted me back to reality as the airline attendant called for plane boarding. The prompt, orderly world I was accustomed to flowed into action as the line of early morning commuters moved through the gate onto the airplane. There were deals to make and money to be made. In moments, we would trust our lives to the integrity of that craft to carry us thousands of feet above the earth to Frankfurt.

Back in India, I know a man whose integrity will carry him high and far to his God-given destination, too.

P.S. Oh, yes, I spoke to Awan's mentor, and was given his smiling agreement to bless him with the earrings. I told him, "He is a man you can cross any river with. I know, because I have friends like that back home."

—68—

The LORD God is my strength, and he will
make my feet like hinds' feet,
and he will make me to walk upon mine high places.
—Habakkuk 3:19 (KJV)

The leap looked impossible. Sheer, rugged, rock cliffs marked a thousand-foot drop into a dark abyss. A ripping wind cut sharply around the jagged, icy lips of the cliff edge.

Snow rode on the wind, covered ancient cracks and crevices, and whipped in swirling cadence before it released its stingy grip on a handful of flakes, and flinged them over the edge into oblivion. The storm roared and howled, and the ice stung like swarms of bees.

The old billy goat stood back from the cliff's edge and pondered the leap, calculating the launch. Muscles tensed, his sturdy hind legs launched him forward as his hooves gripped the icy rock, feeling for maximum purchase of the available traction. His body bolted forward, head down, eyes focused, he covered the short distance to the precipice in seconds. When his front hooves touched the point of no return, he launched himself with full might into thin air.

My eyes moved down the painting, carefully following the detailed use of texture, light and shadow until my gaze fixed on the caption. *"Faith."*

I studied the word for a moment and then raised my eyes again to study the billy goat, fixed in mid-air nothingness. From matter to matter he flew. Did he make it? I followed the trajectory of his body on the painting. *Yes*, I thought to myself, *he did make it.*

But that's not the point, is it? Faith is the willingness to take the risk of leap, embrace the invisible, and jump away from the safety of what matters to what really matters. Those who hang back in fear will never know the outcome -- or even understand the leap.

As I studied the billy more closely, I noticed how deliberate he was. The artist had somehow captured the essence of real faith, and how it always produces action. And action in its turn, when taken with faith in God, always produces a blessing.

Perhaps this goat was teaching me even a deeper lesson. I continued to study the painting, wondering about the other side… the blessing just across the abyss. I thought of men and women in the Bible and the leaps of faith many of them had taken. My mind traced the lives of people I know, and even a few small leaps of my own.

It all hinges on how we interpret the prospect of a blessing. A blessing is not always simple, trouble-free, risk-free, or even down-to-earth easy. More often than not, a blessing awaits us on the other side of those dark and mysterious leaps of faith -- usually accompanied by poor footing, unruly circumstances, limited visibility, and an unknown outcome. But not completely unknown, because Jesus is always there to meet you.

I reached up, carefully removed the painting from the store wall, and went to the checkout register.

Billy was going home with me.

—69—

*"Be strong and very courageous. Be careful to obey all
the instructions Moses gave you. Do not deviate from
them, turning either to the right or to the left.
Then you will be successful in everything you do."*
—*Joshua 1:7 (NLT)*

Standing on top of Cliffty Mountain made my head swim
and my knees wobble. Peaking out at just less than seven
thousand feet high, Cliffty bears a well-earned name. A
mere eighteen inches from the end of my big toes was a sheer
drop off of a couple thousand feet.

I breathed deeply and raised my eyes, and casted my vision
due north up the pristine expanse of the Kootenai River Valley,
where the river seemed to disappear into the mountains of
British Columbia.

Carefully, I turned with the compass, facing each direction.
To the west laid the dark shadows of the Selkirk Mountains, to the
north and east, the Purcells stood as sentinels on the Montana
state line. I stood in the Cabinet Mountains, which broke away
to the southeast like the spiny backbone of a dinosaur.

Turning three hundred and sixty degrees, for as far as I
could see, there were mountains. Creator God has always used
the mountains to forge and refine His servants. From thirty
thousand feet in a Boeing jet, mountains appear harmless,
sterile, and small. However, when the unprepared touch their

basalt sides and granite shoulders, they can quickly grind a man into dust.

I'm thinking of mountains with names born on ancient tongues... like Pisgah, Gilead, Ararat, and Carmel. I'm calling to mind desolate heights and wind blistered crags such as Bashan, Gilboa, Sinai, Hachilah, and Nebo. I'm recalling peaks where God fired the spirits of His servants with life, while sanding down their very souls... mountains called Ebal, Hermon and Gerizim.

And what words could I express to add to the loftiness of the Mount of Olives, or the hill called Calvary?

God's mountaintop forge produces a man that is both courageous and careful. Joshua was one such man. Repeatedly, the Bible says that Joshua "had a different spirit." Different in the way he looked at God, and different in the way he viewed obstacles and problems. Joshua had been educated on desolate peaks at the side of Moses.

Outnumbered, yet not outgunned by a disbelieving majority who insisted on allowing their view of God to be blocked by obstacles, Joshua unflinchingly fixed his eyes on God, who gave him a clear vision of the promise.

Three times in Joshua 1 we discover God commanding Joshua to be strong and courageous. Two times, God commands Joshua to "observe" to do... all that was written in the law. Another word for observe is the English word "careful."

Courageous and careful describe God's prescription for success in life. Sounds like the character ingredients for climbing mountains, doesn't it?

Take courage friends, and be careful out there. God wants all of us to reach the top and take in the view.

"Be wary of false preachers who smile a lot, dripping with practiced sincerity. Chances are they are out to rip you off some way or other. Don't be impressed with charisma; look for character. Who preachers are is the main thing, not what they say. A genuine leader will never exploit your emotions or your pocketbook."
—Matthew 7:15 (MSG)

The poet Edgar Guest wrote,
> I have to live with myself, and so,
> I want to be fit for myself to know;
> I want to be able as days go by,
> Always to look myself straight in the eye;
> I don't want to stand with the setting sun
> And hate myself for the things I've done.
>
> I don't want to keep on a closet shelf
> A lot of secrets about myself,
> And fool myself as I come and go
> Into thinking that nobody else will know
> The kind of man I really am;
> I don't want to dress myself up in sham.

Picture a single candle, its flame burning bright in an inky black night. That's the best picture I can think of to illustrate the need of the hour -- authentic, godly character in these spiritually dark and desperate days.

Nothing is more valuable to you or those you serve and love than your character. No matter how high you climb the ladder of success, if it's leaning against a wall of compromise and you lose your character in the pursuit, you have lost *everything*.

Recently I came across an article, which originated in Israel, describing the characteristics of a cult. As I read over the piece, it occurred to me that the warning signs of following a pseudo-leader into a false belief system (a house of cards) are the small flashing lights and sometimes faint alarm bells of a compromised character.

One identifying mark of this sort of leader is an excessively dominant style. Little by little, this flawed, insecure character gains a degree of influence, which controls many, if not most, of the decisions that effect the lives of the followers. As a result, the leader is followed blindly and without question.

When a community of believers are healthy and life giving, they freely and openly recognize and respect a leader's spiritual authority. Followers choose to follow because they trust the leader and the leadership team. And why do they trust? Because they see and recognize the character of Jesus flowing from the leaders' lives, which comes from the fruit of the Spirit.

There is moral accountability, which produces life and health in the followers, as opposed to fear, shame, and guilt. *There is a big difference between preaching moral conviction and exerting manipulative control.*

Jesus told us that He came to give us "life and life more abundantly" whereas the devil comes to "steal, kill and destroy" (John 10:10). In the devil's temptation of Christ, he challenged Him to jump off the temple roof. That is evil.

I have often said through the years that authentic, biblical Christianity is the only religion where you are not required to leave your brain in the trunk of your car. No doubt you perceive that I feel a great deal of passion over this, and for good reason. I am made of the same stuff as any leader, so I am not writing with a sense of superiority or an "I-have-it-all-together" arrogance.

Our times are complicated, complex, and confusing. Our challenge has never been greater or our cause for Christ more vital. Moreover, in these convoluted days, it is easy for any leader to forget that Jesus washed feet and rode on a donkey. As one sage stated, "It is character that counts."

Whether you lead a family, a business, or a church, the temptation to (compromise) and complain comes easy. Thank God for the tough times. They're the reason you're there -- to be the leader. If everything was going well you wouldn't be needed. When the tough calls must be made, your confidence can be found in these words: "The LORD is on my side; I will not fear...." (Psalm 118:6, NKJV).

—71—

In the Messiah we give off a sweet scent rising to God,
which is recognized by those on the way of salvation—an
aroma redolent with life. But those on the way to destruction
treat us more like the stench from a rotting corpse.
—*2 Corinthians 2:14-16 (MSG)*

Foul, odious, putrid, rank and a revolting stench unlike anything I can recall.... and it was coming from our garage. *Where? What? Uggh! Phew!* I had to find the source of that squalid smell.

Having a strong nose is more than merely the asset of a built-in compass; it is also an appendage that requires superior maintenance and attention because of its high sensitivity. This led me on the hunt to Eli... our tri-color Border collie with deep roots in Scotland. For all his high breeding, he is a low class varmint. Or should I say what he found was a varmint in the form of a dead raccoon in our back yard, in the city, no less and the carcass was just rotten enough to have the consistency of a poached egg.

Eli had skillfully taken the rotted corpse and strategically laid it in the lawn of our backyard where he had tactfully begun rubbing, stroking and massaging from the bottom of his chin down his throat to the front of his chest until he was completely covered with a shiny, greasy gloss.

And the odor? Well, it would have made a black fly retch. After that he went to our garage where his kennel was located and took a leisurely nap until the entire place was unbearable.

That's when I walked in. Earlier, I had watched him from the kitchen window, wondering why he appeared to have a shiny gloss to his coat as if he had been rubbed down with expensive oriental oil. *That's odd, I thought, He was smiling, too.*

An animal activist would have imprisoned me had they known what I was thinking as I now looked at Eli, delightfully dreaming as he dozed. After all, I am a gun owner... he wouldn't know what... ok, that is not an option... but it did cross my mind more than once.

After my son, Ethan, gave Eli two aggressive and brisk shampooing baths with steaming hot, sudsy water, a shampoo that would strip paint off a wall and the garden hose, he was beginning to be tolerable. I said beginning to be... after that, all he wanted to do was play. He felt great and frisky, the rotten mutt.

After I had disposed of his dead play pal, I thought about how our American culture has changed since I was a boy. As a benchmark, let's use 1962 and consider how our culture has changed concerning their view of God, Jesus, the church, Christians and Christmas.

Guess what? Not much has changed since Paul wrote those words to the Corinthian church way back in the first century. "Those on the way to destruction treat us more like the stench from a rotting corpse."

What really matters this Christmas is that "in the Messiah, in Christ, God leads us from place to place in one perpetual victory parade. Through us, he brings knowledge of Christ. Everywhere we go, people breathe in the exquisite fragrance. Because of Christ, we give off a sweet scent rising to God, which is recognized by those on the way of salvation -- an aroma redolent with life."

That is something to celebrate.

—72—

*"Cut the living child in two, and give half to
one woman and half to the other!"*
—1 Kings 3:25 (NLT)

King Solomon pondered the two women standing before him. His lingering silence thickened the air, already electric with emotion. As the two mothers poured out their hearts -- their words bursting with fear, anger, and sorrow -- the king listened, considered, and prayed.

Here were two mothers and two infants who had been sharing the same room, when the unthinkable happened. One baby accidentally smothered during the night.

Now both moms, with deep anguish and tears, stood before the throne, each one claimed the remaining child as her own. The king made the judgment, but without the benefit of DNA evidence, CSI reports, or collaborating witness testimony. Only the two mothers possessed firsthand knowledge of what really happened in the night. *And one of them was lying.*

Before he spoke, Solomon wrestled with questions that forced themselves to the surface of his mind: "If I were the true mother of this remaining child, what would I most care about? What overarching motive would drive me in this moment?"

Solomon silently prayed, "Give me wisdom, Lord."

The answer was there in precisely the moment he asked the question; almost imperceptibly it filled his heart and his mind. His words were measured and his tone even as he spoke.

"Bring me a sword," he said. "Cut the living child in two, and give half to one and half to the other."

Suddenly, the mother of the living child shrieked, crying, "*No!* I can't bear the thought of my child cut into two pieces. Give her the baby." Falling to her knees she pleaded, "Whatever you do, don't kill him."

Solomon called on his attendants to help her up. He recognized that only a genuine mother's love would so willingly hand her baby over to another woman rather than have the child harmed in any way. When he looked at her (with a smile, perhaps?), Solomon said, "The baby is yours. Take him and go in peace."

I have learned a small measure about the Father heart of God. You might refer to this as the heart of the Good Shepherd. It is magnificently expressed in this biblical account of a mother's heart. There is great and eternal value in this story for pastors, elders, deacons, and church leaders, although the principles learned could be applied to presidents and parents.

For the real mother, the most important thing in this story was the child. The story is about the baby -- not the woman's ability to prove she was the child's biological mother, nor her power to win ultimate possession of the infant. She was not driven by power, control, jealousy, or even fear. This mother was moved by sacrificial love. Love that was willing to let go for the sake of life, rather than control, ending in death.

On the other hand, I have to wonder how many church splits have divided a local congregation where the heart of the Good Shepherd was absent in the leadership. I'm speaking of people who -- in their anger and indignation -- have been willing to follow through with the sword of division, while saying, "If I can't have it and control it, I will cut it in two." This action, of course, kills relationships and life fades.

In this specific set of circumstances, it doesn't take long to discern, as Solomon did, who *really* loves the church -- or the small group or the ministry or ministry team. The kind of cutting, dividing, and splitting I am referring to can happen in a nation or a county seat. And it can most certainly grasp a business or a family. In its ultimate manifestation, we see King Herod in Matthew chapter two, who was willing to put any number of innocents to the sword rather than consider even a God-ordained threat to his own position.

This willingness to divide and kill drives Jesus out of the very places and relationships where we most desperately need Him to live and reside.

What will you do with the baby?

—73—

"The very words I have spoken to you are spirit and life....
Are you also going to leave?" Jesus asked. Simon Peter replied,
"Lord, to whom would we go? You have the words that give eternal
life. We believe, and we know you are the Holy One of God."
—John 6:63, 67-68 (NLT)

Indiana Jones says, "X never marks the spot!" Having invested so much of his life digging through ancient piles of stony rubble in search of treasures, I think Indy ought to know.

The first time I walked the narrow, stone passageways of the old city of Jerusalem was in 1985. Since then, Israel has experienced the fiery test of change, both internally and under scrutiny on the world stage.

Looking at the ancient stones in this place, you can't help but feel awed by the thousands of people -- both worshipers and warriors -- who have coursed across their surface. A few days ago, my friend, Tom Hall, and I worked our way up into the city of David in intense heat. We traversed the old city wall on the south, moving around to the eastern wall paralleling the Kidron Valley. To my right were the Mount of Olives and the Garden of Gethsemane. To my left was the old city wall where we came upon the closed Eastern Gate, filled in with stone and mortar. This is where tradition says the Messiah will one day enter the city, ascending Temple Mount and reestablishing the throne of David.

My senses were in overdrive with all the spiritual history represented within a stone's throw to my left and right. I thought of Nehemiah's description upon his inspection of the walls of the city five hundred years before Christ. "Rubble" was his assessment. In and among these stones, geologists, archeologists, and scholars have dug and are still digging to unearth the secrets of their history and the treasures hidden therein.

The worshipers and the warriors still come to walk over these very old pavements, some in search of the visible and tangible, and others for the spiritual and otherworldly. There's no doubt that people visiting the old city -- and other sites in Israel -- feel a measure of comfort, just reflecting on the fact that they have "walked where Jesus walked." I have felt it, too. He's really no nearer to me here, than He is in northern Idaho... but there is something stirring about the knowledge that when Jesus walked this earth in the flesh, He put His sandaled feet down on some of these very streets.

The truth is, no one can say with any degree of certainty, that He stood exactly here, ate a meal precisely there, or taught a message in this or that very spot. History, war, and the long press of time has heaped the rubble deeper and deeper, one pile upon another, until it's all but impossible to orientate one's faith in Jesus with locations in the land where He once walked.

This is why -- even though we would probably all find a visit to the Holy Land a stirring thing to do -- our faith must rest on the Word of God and nothing else, except by the Holy Spirit's guidance.

Tom and I made our way past the western wall and once again ascended Mount Zion. And as we did, one thought was uppermost in my heart: Physical locations may be significant but historical sites cannot replace the Savior, nor can ancient places fill the human soul like the Prince of Peace can. Jesus Himself said that His words are spirit and life and like Peter, where could we go? Who else has the words of eternal life?

The location is not the main thing; His life is the main thing. The life we receive in Jesus is the main thing.

Tom and I walked out through Jaffa Gate, passed the Tower of David and all my sensory stimulation was still in high gear. I love the history of it all, I really do.

However, when it comes to where "X" marks the spot for Jesus, only your heart will do.

—74—

"Nail him to a cross!"
—Matthew 27:22 (MSG)

The old man's eyes narrowed into black ink dots, even more so as he stroked his muti, filled with bones, monkey teeth, and assorted other shaman attachments.

"I will sell you my house... on one condition," he rasped.

"What condition?" Masozi responded. "You know I have the money to pay you. My wife and children need a place to live. Sell me the house! What is your condition? I will meet it, whatever it is."

"There is nail driven in the wood above the door. I will sell you the house and you will own everything... except that nail. *"The nail belongs to me."*

Masozi did not flinch or even pause to think about his barter. *What is one nail?* He thought to himself. *The old man has lived in his world of dark magic too long. One nail means nothing to my family and me.*

"Very well," Masozi replied. "The nail is yours, the house is mine."

His leathery face wrinkling in a smile, the old man simply said, "Good."

A year later, Masozi, weary from the day's work, was happy to be walking up to his house. Hearing his approach, his wife ran down the path to meet him. She was upset, waving her arms.

"Masozi, Masozi, the old man who sold you the house came by today. He hung a *dead dog* above the door of our house!"

Sure enough, as Masozi stood in front of his house, his eyes fixed above the door, there hanging on the old man's nail was a dead dog. Masozi ran quickly to where the old man lived. He seemed to be waiting for Masozi, seated in front of his house on a stool.

"What have you done?" Masozi cried. "You cannot hang a dead dog over our front door!"

"Oh, but I can," the old man responded. "You agreed, the nail belongs to me. The dog is hanging on my nail."

Masozi hung his head and returned home with the terrible news. The old man was correct. He had made a deal without thinking about the consequences of his decision. Within days the carcass was putrid and the odor unbearable. Masozi knew he had made a deal with the devil, and the only action he could take was to move his family out of the house.

Someone once said that if you give the devil just a glimpse of your heart, he will nail you. *Have you ever been nailed?* I have, and it hurts. Here's the good news... Jesus got nailed so you wouldn't have to. That must have been what Paul meant when he wrote: "Do not give the devil that kind of foothold (or opportunity) in your life" (Ephesians 4:27).

Or, I would add, a way to nail you.

—75—

"As an eagle stirs up its nest,
Hovers over its young,
Spreading out its wings, taking them up,
Carrying them on its wings,
*So the L*ORD *alone led him...."*
—Deuteronomy 32:11-12 (NKJV)

Have you ever noticed how Father God loves to surprise you when you least expect it? Just yesterday, my wife and I were busy working in the yard, preparing to move. I'm almost certain that we didn't walk out the door saying to each other, "You know honey, I think the Holy Spirit is going to say something to us while we're working in the yard."

But He did, and we were surprised by it all. As we cruised around the house, enjoying the smell of honeysuckle, lavender, and roses, we immediately noticed clumps of debris covering the front lawn. Stuff like balls of hair, large sticks of varying lengths, pieces of fabric, twine, and assorted other items.

About the same time, the air was filled with the loud cries, caws, and shrieks from a pair of large ebony black ravens, which have been nesting in one of the pine trees for the past month and a half. They carried on like Attila the Hun had just entered their domain. There was a spot under the tree where there was a more dense concentration of odds and ends. From that point the spread of debris reached out in a radius of perhaps twenty feet. I stood under the pine and peered up through the branches, dodging the piercing rays of sunlight. Using existing limbs as a sun block, I found a position where I could see up and into where these black loudmouths had nested. To my amazement I saw two nearly-grown young ravens perched on limbs, and as quiet as mannequins -- unlike their two obnoxious parents who saw us as a threat.

As I studied them, I noticed the area where the nest had been. Only a few scraps of material remained. Then it dawned on me. They are like eagles in that they don't kick their young out of the nest, they slowly and meticulously dismantle the nest until any vestiges of comfort or convenience for the young are gone. Why? So their young will take the risk and fly. That's right. They want their young to fly the coop, take a leap and dive into thin air. Funny thing is, if God had not put that into the parent ravens, the young would have been completely content to set in the nest and wait for mom and dad to hand, well, in this case, beak feed them.

But eagles and ravens and other birds that soar the warm air currents were meant to fly. They would never see what they were meant to see, sitting in a nest. They would never feel those feathers of flight utilize a greater law than gravity, the law of flight to lift them to new heights as their wings stretched out to the maximum, reaching those dizzy heights.

The parents had intentionally dismantled their supposed comfort zone because it would eventually destroy them. Did you observe in the verse above that it says God Himself stirs up the nest of His people? He dismantles our comfort zones. Why? Because we were meant to fly to new altitudes and attitudes, not perch in old, crusty nests that only become worsened by the wear -- in fact, downright nasty.

The Hebrew word for "stir" conveys the idea of "opening the eyes," "to wake," and "to stir up." God messes with our stuff to wake us up to the new and lofty heights He wants to take us to. *But we must be willing to leave the nest.* The place that He built in the past and provided for us must be a launching pad, not a mausoleum that we memorialize forever.

He says, "No way! I have bigger plans for you than that. I am going to take you to a viewpoint that will 'stir up' and 'awaken' My vision for your life. I want you to see so much more than the balls of hair, sticks, and fabric that you have called home. Now is the time to fly… so I'm making your world uncomfortable until you are willing to leave the nest."

Eagles go a step further coaxing their young to fly, literally dropping them out of the nest into thin air, and then staying close to catch them if they freeze up and fall. In the same way, God will never allow us to hit the ground, but carries us on His wings.

Bottom line: the Holy Spirit spoke to us, saying, *"Don't be afraid to leave your nest. Come fly with Me."*

Who said yard work isn't spiritual?

—76—

"Look! The Lamb of God who takes away the sin of the world!"
—John 1:29-30 (NLT)

The term "High Holidays" refers to Rosh Hashanah (the Jewish New Year) and Yom Kippur together. Yom Kippur, which literally means "the day of atonement," concludes the Ten Days of Awe. For Jews, it is the holiest and most somber day of the year (Leviticus 23:27-32).

In ancient times, one day each year, the high priest entered the Holy of Holies to put the blood of the sacrificed animal on the altar as a sin offering. In faith and in obedience to God's precise instructions, His people experienced atonement, or covering, for sin.

Today, Yom Kippur is a day of fasting and reflecting upon one's sin.

A number of years ago we were working with a foreign attorney to secure legitimacy for Global Gateway Network in that nation. Through a series of events, I learned that this attorney had embezzled funds we had targeted for the legal process. As it turned out, there was little we could do about the theft, and the lawyer told me so point blank. Nancy, the team, and I began to pray every day for the redemption of this situation. More specifically, we prayed for the attorney to have a change of heart.

I will never forget being seated in worship at Faith Assembly on a Sunday morning, and receiving an e-mail on my smart phone. In the nation where the lawyer lived, it was Monday. On Sunday, she had attended an international church where the speaker taught on Yom Kippur, and how Jesus became our ultimate sacrifice (John 1:29). She became deeply convicted of her theft and fraud. In response, she repented and emailed me these words:

Dear Micah,

Times pass on and we come on the Rosh Hashana, the Jewish New Year. Today is the tenth day, entering the Yom Kippur. I examine myself. I want to be right before God and before you as my brother in Christ. I did sin and I want to confess to you Micah regarding the fund. I will return the money. Please forgive me. I'm so sorry... Micah!

Thank you.

She returned every penny! When repentance engages redemption, there is no power, visible or invisible, that can stop forgiveness!

Yom Kippur reminds us that we can forgive and be forgiven in Christ.

Yom Kippur signals a fresh start, new beginnings and a clean slate in life. What a great deal.

Shana Tova!

—77—

If you help the poor, you are lending to the LORD
and He will repay you!
—Proverbs 19:17 (NLT)

Christmas in North Vietnam feels different than Christmas at home. It was the Christmas season, when my daughter, Andrea, and I traveled with Global Gateway Network's first team to visit the Center of Hope, home for children.

Just nine months prior, in March 2003, Robert Armstrong and I had prayer walked a bare hill top in Loc Binh village, about 4 miles from the border of China, asking God to help us, help the children of the region.

Miraculously, our negotiations with the Government of Vietnam settled on a plan, we raised the money to build the facility and the team is ready to dedicate the property and forty eight children, under our care.

Having been raised in the Pacific Northwest, I have a particular cultural idea of what Christmas time looks like, feels like, smells like and especially what Christmas time tastes like.

Simple things like fir trees covered in bright, festive decorations and colored lights and happy tinsel. I think about nativity scenes and candles and joyful songs. I can see snow men and reindeer and a jolly man dressed in a red suit with a zillion weary parents lined up with children who are not sure if they want to talk to him or not. I can almost smell Hannah's sugar cookies covered with gooey icing and taste the candy canes full of peppermint. All of these traditions point me to one single truth, *"I am loved and valued."*

From where I sit at this present moment, I cannot see or feel or smell or taste any of those special Christmas treasures. Nonetheless, I do know I am loved and valued even in the most unfamiliar and, in some instances, unfriendly of settings.

I have a two page list of more than 4000 items the team brought to Center of Hope.

Time and space will not allow me to list them all but indulge me as I share a few of the gifts we delivered: fifty five beanie babies, fifty seven teddy bears, two hundred seventy five single hair clips and barrettes, four soccer balls, eighteen jump ropes, eighty blankets, fourteen yo-yos, nine sets of jacks, thirty rubber balls, four flutes, sixty one bars of soap, seventy one boxes of colored pencils, eighteen puzzles, sixty eight boxes of crayons, three hundred seventy two tootsie pops, two hundred six pairs of socks, one hundred seventeen t-shirts, one hundred ninety seven sets of underwear, nine bottles of shampoo, boxes of schools supplies, sewing supplies, medicine and on and on it could go.

Because of the communist government's oppressive control and the not so secret police with us, we cannot gather all the children together and have a Sunday school class, telling them about the life, death and resurrection of Jesus.

What we did and will continue to do is demonstrate through deed and action "you are loved and valued," by Jesus and us. I have learned that there are many ways one can be poor in this life. It is not merely a monetary issue. This holy season, why don't you tell – no, better yet -- do something for someone who is somehow living poorly that will show them "you are loved and valued." That is the real meaning of Christmas, don't you agree?

Now have those sugar cookies ready when I get home!

Post Script: I wrote this piece in December of 2003. By 2006, we were allowed to bring books, DVD's and other Christian material to the children. During this time, our team members were able to lead twenty-three of the children and three staff members to Christ. Since 2003, Global Gateway Network sent more than twenty-five teams to Center of Hope, the largest a medical team of thirty-five members. We delivered hundreds of thousands of dollars of medical and humanitarian supplies to the Loc Binh area. By 2011, persecution of Christians began to intensify and our ability to work was greatly diminished and limited. We continue to pray and seek ways to help the hill tribal people, especially the children of Loc Binh.

—78—

I used to wander off until you disciplined me;
but now I closely follow your word.
—Psalm 119:67 (NLT)

My troubles turned out all for the best—
they forced me to learn from your textbook.
—Psalm 119:71 (MSG)

Wandering is a natural human tendency. During the years that Nancy and I had arms full of toddlers, we experienced panic on more than one occasion because of wandering. The only thing one of our kiddos needed to escape was a mere moment of a turned head... and in a flash they were gone.

Thank God, we always found them quickly, which was followed by a huge sigh of relief that they were safe and back in our arms. A good talking to about the merits of staying with mom and dad followed, along with remarks detailing all the evils in the world, when one wanders off.

I've since discovered that wandering off is also an adult practice. Even though Father God is the only perfect parent ever, we human kids still have that natural inclination to wander off. But being the good dad that He is, He finds us, deals with us and brings us home, if we allow Him to do so.

Make no mistake, Father God is more committed to bring back the wandering one than you are. Should we pray for them?

Absolutely! Should we continue to love them? YES! Should we accept them? Without doubt.

I understand how easy it is to confuse acceptance with approval.

Then there is temptation to bail your loved one out of a dilemma. It is strong... but it requires discernment. Premature comfort does nothing to heal the wound. Every leader, every pastor, every healer, (that includes parents) must be alert to the dangers of premature comfort.

Denise Levertov's caution is worth heeding: "Yet the fear nags me: is the wound my life has suffered healing too fast, shutting in bad blood? Will the scar pucker the skin of my soul?"

The ancient phrase *Pathemata mathemata* (suffered things are learned things) is true. The pressure of pain produces communion with Father God when we run to Him... not from Him.

Remember that the prodigal came to his senses in a pigpen not a palace.... and the Father waited.

—79—

*Those of us who are strong and able in the faith need to
step in and lend a hand to those who falter, and not just
do what is most convenient for us. Strength is for service,
not status. Each one of us needs to look after the good of the
people around us, asking ourselves, "How can I help?"*
—Romans 15:1-2 (MSG)

Have you ever walked into one of those huge, cavernous warehouses that specialize in making you run a complete marathon before you find someone to offer help or service? I have and on especially cold days I have been known to put on my running gear, drive to one of those huge indoor labyrinths and do my long distance mileage for the week. Why? Because I know no one will bother me.

Well, that is fine and dandy for a work out, but it doesn't help the company serve the community and it certainly doesn't fulfill their mission, now does it?

This is especially troubling for people who walk in hoping to receive some help rebuilding their house which burned down by fire or was blown over by wind or watered down by a broken pipe or rain storm connected to a bad roof job.

When I was a small boy riding in our family car with my mom, she would drive into a *service* station to buy some gasoline, and suddenly two or three guys appeared out of nowhere asking if they could check this while going over that as they washed the windows and checked the air in tires.

As time passed and I begin to drive, I noticed that when I pulled into a gas station that I was given a choice of self-serve or full service based upon how much I wanted to pay per gallon of gas. These days, it's all *self-serve* and the price is higher than ever in our history. Too bad, isn't it? The death of good service, I mean. No doubt, good service suffered the same demise as common sense in America; in a head-on collision with self-centeredness.

What is even more tragic is this whole self-serve madness has infiltrated the church. Every week people, men, women, boys and girls, walk into church buildings across America running on fumes, deflated and unable to see because of obscured vision. Even new people come through our doors because their lives are burning down or their families are blown away. They feel soaked by the storm. Like those big manufactured warehouses and well-lit gas stations, we can put up nice signs and offer slick publications in our churches but there is no substitute for a warm smile, a welcoming handshake and words like, "How can I help you?" A few invested moments eye to eye with another human being, sharing that kind of loving, hospitable, service in our self-serving world has the potential to change someone's eternity.

People need Jesus, serve them.

—80—

Draw close to God, and God will draw close to you.
Wash your hands, you sinners; purify your hearts....
—James 4:8 (NLT)

Have you noticed how the buzz about hand washing goes through cycles every few years? On more than one occasion, the matter reached critical mass on cruise ships down in Florida.

What more than one thousand vacationers had hoped would be a memorable cruise turned into microbial curse. The upshot of the whole messy experience is everyone on board learned a new handshake or should I say, elbow shake.

I am not a little intrigued by the fact that a simple thing like hand washing could be so potent against unseen microbes. On the other hand, I am equally riveted to the "society of microbiology's " survey that reveals "While ninety five percent of men and women surveyed say they wash their hands after using a public restroom, only sixty seven percent of people actually do wash before leaving the restroom."

It appears many Americans have forgotten the single best piece of infection control advice Mom ever gave them – "always wash your hands after you go to the bathroom."

I know, I know, it *does* seem silly to write about something we've been told for as long as we can remember. Don't hit the delete button just yet; I believe I can capture something of Heaven's heart in this matter. The plain truth is people get

11

sick from touching and tasting germ-infected nouns. Mom was right, soap will protect you and I from microbes, but soap won't protect your heart.

Reminds me of Proverbs 4:23, "Above all else, guard your heart, for it affects everything you do." Throughout history people have attempted to deal with heart issues by washing their hands, which in essence is saying, "I'm washing my hands of you," or "I'm washing my hands of this!"

For example, when Pilate saw that he was getting nowhere and that a riot was imminent, he took a basin of water and washed his hands in full sight of the crowd, saying, "I'm washing my hands of responsibility for this man's death. From now on, it's in your hands" (Matthew 27:24). And of course, it didn't wash.

Even Job knew washing his hands would not cleanse his heart. "Even if I wash myself with the strongest soap I can find, it wouldn't last". Job 9:29-30

The single best piece of infection advice God has given us for our hearts is from "the man after His own heart." Remember David's words in these days of infection: "Create in me a clean heart, O God" Psalm 51:10 (NKJV).

Go ahead, scrub up and don't forget those fingernails.

—81—

On the final and climactic day of the Feast, Jesus took his stand.
He cried out, "If anyone thirsts, let him come to me and drink.
Rivers of living water will brim and spill out of the depths of
anyone who believes in Me this way, just as the Scripture says."
—John 7:37-38 (MSG)

The term "burnout" is relatively new and unique to our culture. And the baby boom generation in particular. I wonder about that, don't you? Especially in light of the fact that we have so many things that supposedly make our lives easier.

In recent years there have been a plethora of afflictions which people suffer with connected to weariness. Things like chronic fatigue syndrome or myalgic encephalomyelitis and fibromyalgia come to mind. The medical community is finally taking notice of these maladies. However, there is little they can do. And yet, it appears to be epidemic. The pain and weariness accompanied by guilt weighs heavily on many a soul.

A friend responded to this condition one time and said, "I am tired of living and afraid of dying." Too many of God's kids can identify with that feeling.

He frequently targeted people who were just plain tired. In Matthew 11:28-30, Jesus said, "Are you tired? Worn out? Burned out on religion? Come to me. Get away with me and you'll recover your life. I'll show you how to take a real rest. Walk with me and work with me -- watch how I do it. Learn the unforced rhythms of grace. I won't lay anything heavy or ill fitting on you. Keep company with me and you'll learn to live freely and lightly."

I don't know the origin of this old story but it bears repeating. One day a man was walking across a large, open pasture. Reaching the other side, he approached a cabin. As he passed by the cabin, he saw what looked like a man pumping feverishly at a hand pump. The man's arms worked at terrific speed and pace, not slowing down one bit. Pumping on and on, up and down, he appeared tireless. As the man watched, he couldn't believe what he was seeing, so he moved closer to the cabin and the man pumping from the well. Easing ever closer, it finally became clear to him that it was not a man at the pump, but a wooden silhouette figure painted to look like a man. The arm that was pumping so rapidly was hinged at the elbow and wired to the pump handle.

The water surged out of the spout with powerful force, not because the figure was pumping it, but because it was an artesian well. *The water was pumping the man.*

Perhaps with all of our technological advancement and material success this is one essential thing we have gotten backwards. Falsely believing it is our strength that produces, when all the time the Holy Spirit is available as river of living water.

All we have to do is keep our hand on the handle.

—82—

"And no one puts new wine into old wineskins."
—Luke 5:37-38 (NLT)

The world is always changing. And without man's permission, I might add. Change is rarely easy and often filled with chaos. And great opportunity if we are nimble and willing to adjust our methods. One of the most stark examples I've witness was in 2002, when

Nancy, Hannah, Ethan and I traveled to Germany with a front row seat to a really historical change. Twelve European countries have launched the largest financial change in world history. Each one has agreed to abandon their national currency for a common note called the euro. Think of this: some three hundred million Europeans, from the Arctic Circle to the fringes of Africa, will be impacted by this change. It doesn't appear to me that Germans are all that happy about the currency change. Ireland's punt, or pound, has been around since 1928. What is more, the drachma in Greece has a history that goes back some 2,500 years. This has been a monumental change because they all ceased to exist in March 2002.

When Jesus told the parable of new wine recorded by Luke, there were no glass or plastic bottles available for wide spread use. In those days, people would pour their drinks into animal skins that were sewn together and used like canteens. Over time these skins would lose their elasticity and become brittle.

Eventually, they would break and become useless. Their tender capacity to contain was diminished.

Jesus used the wineskin to teach us about resilience and change. He said, "New wine must be poured into new wineskins." This is a life principle: new situations always require new structures. A new job often requires you to learn new skills. A new relationship often requires new ways of relating.

What are your old wineskins? Old ways of thinking? Old habits? They could be outdated ways of acting, talking, or responding that worked well in the past, but aren't useful or helpful anymore. Will you hold on to old wineskins or will you abandon them for new ones?

The Bible says, "The intelligent man is always open to new ideas, in fact, he looks for them" (Proverbs 18:15, TLB).

Pause with me right now and ask Jesus what new wine is He pouring into your Life. *A tender wineskin is always full.*

—83—

"Have you heard the way Jesus talks? We've
never heard anyone speak like Him."
—John 7:46 (MSG)

We sometimes pretend that words don't mean much, but they are incredibly powerful and potent. I recall the law of words as a boy... "Sticks and stones can break my bones but words can never hurt me." Never hurt me... you've got to be kidding! Our words curse or consecrate, wound or heal. Our words are infused with the power to release blessing or blight, life or death. Words can break a child's heart... destroy a husband's dreams... tear down a wife's self-respect...ruin a local church.

A survey taken of Americans revealed the three most common word phrases we love to hear: *"I love you." "I forgive you." And "supper is ready."*

I like that. We can change another person's life with these simple words? What about words like, "Great job," or "You'll make it through this," or "I trust you," or "The truth is..."

Words are like bricks. You can use them to smash a window or you can use them to build a foundation. We get to choose, every day, how we'll utilize this incredibly powerful gift that we've been given by Father God.

As I think about building I remember the Old Testament story of the tower of Babel. Here you discover how and why Father God righteously halted their building project. Genesis eleven unveils the Babel blueprint for a tower so high that the friends and family began to fall apart because of pride.

To stop the project, God took away their most important tool. Surprisingly, it wasn't the engineer's compass or the carpenter's hammer or chisel; He took away their ability to communicate.

Consequently, people were fragmented; families, friends, co-workers and neighbors unraveled into segmented camps of isolation, spinning off across the continent. But that is not the end of the story. Acts chapter two records the restoration of communication. The hinge point was the arrival of the Holy Spirit with full flow of Heaven's heart to heal people, restore families and mend the breach of communication.

Do you recall the first evidence of the Holy Spirit's arrival? It was words. Nothing less than the ability to communicate like Jesus does. Spirit-fired words carried on the wind of God's presence. Luke collared the moment when he recorded the event:

> They were completely amazed. "How can this be?" they exclaimed. "These people are all from Galilee, and yet we hear them speaking in our own native languages!" (Acts 2:7-8, NLT)

> *The breath of God consummates the beauty of words.*
> I love you…I forgive you…and supper's ready!

—84—

Don't become partners with those who reject God. How can
you make a partnership out of right and wrong? That's not
partnership; that's war. Is light best friends with dark?
—*2 Corinthians 6:14 (MSG)*

What exactly does Paul mean when he tells us not to be "partners with those who reject God?" Is he commanding us to isolate ourselves from any association with unbelievers? Is he warning us to avoid all public places where we might rub shoulders with pagans, atheists and agnostics? Of course not.

Paul was one of history's greatest missionaries. He loved taking the good news of Jesus Christ to places where it had never been and to men and women who had never heard. Paul took the mandates of Jesus seriously; he knew we are called to be salt and light to an unbelieving world. The apostle's command in 2 Corinthians 6:14 has to be something more precise in nature. The old King James says, "Be ye not unequally yoked together with unbelievers."

I can see a wagon being pulled by two oxen yoked together, bearing the burden of their load. You get the picture.

Paul is warning us in the strongest terms about those close relationships and affections that may form between believer and unbeliever. He's talking about those whom we choose to be our closest friends, or whom we form a business partnership with, or (most significantly) whom we choose to marry.

Why is God concerned about this? He knows that when two people who are supposed to be partners have entirely different spiritual perspectives, the result will inevitably be heartache and conflict. Why open the door to unnecessary battles and bullets? I'm reminded of the whimsical battle described by an unknown author:

A duel was fought between Alexander Shott and John Nott.

Nott was shot and Shott was not.

In this case it is better to be Shott than Nott.

Some said that Nott was not shot.

But Shott says that he shot Nott.

It may be that the shot Shott shot, shot Nott, or it may be possible that the shot Shott shot, shot Shott himself. We think, however, that the shot Shott shot, shot not Shott, but Nott.

Anyway, it is hard to tell which was shot and which was not.

In the words of Winston Churchill, "Nothing is as exhilarating as being shot at and missed."

—85—

The LORD directs the steps of the godly.
He delights in every detail of their lives.
Though they stumble, they will never fall,
for the LORD holds them by the hand.
—Psalm 37:23-24 (NLT)

I remember one dark winter day in 1980 when I was not feeling well. Although there was an unusual church service scheduled in the evening, I had no plans of going. Until my mom called and said, "Son, I know you don't feel well but I believe that God has something special planned for you tonight."

By faith and not feeling I went to that service and met some people who God strategically used in launching me into international ministry six months later.

Another time, one summer day in 1995 when a pastor I highly respected had invited me to his office to hang out and pray. He looked at me and said, "I believe God wants our two churches to merge and you serve as the senior pastor."

It "seemed" to me that this was utterly impossible but by faith and not feeling I joined him in that vision; in less than one month our two churches were merged and the following five years were miraculous.

I remember receiving an invitation from Billy Graham to join ten thousand other leaders from ninety nations in Amsterdam in the summer of 2000.

I had just returned from Zimbabwe and didn't have the money to fly back to Europe for this gathering. It "seemed" to me to be too much time and resource away from my family and the church I served.

Yet, by faith and not feeling, I said, "Lord, if you want me to go I'll go, but I am asking you to provide the money for me to go." In less than twenty-four hours a generous Christian woman emailed me and shared with me that she believed I should go to Amsterdam and she would pay the bill. During that week in Holland, I joined a think tank on unreached people every afternoon and by the end of the week, adopted three unreached people groups.

By unreached I mean a culture or ethnic group that has zero scripture in their tongue or language, zero believers and zero local churches. I adopted one group in the Middle East, one group in Southeast Asia and one group in northern Europe.

Barnes says of Psalm 37:23, "The English word 'ordered' (directed) means to stand erect; to set up; to found; to adjust, fit, direct. The idea here is, that all that pertains to the journey of a man through life is directed, ordered, fitted, or arranged by the Lord. That is, his course of life is under divine guidance and control."

And Matthew Henry writes, "By His grace and Holy Spirit He directs the thoughts, affections, and designs of good men. This is the way, walk in it. He does not always show him his way at a distance, but leads him step by step, as children are led, and so keeps him in a continual dependence upon His guidance."

If you are struggling today with inky darkness and murkiness of feelings and it seems that God has disconnected from you, lift your chin and your eyes because as a skilled archer hits the bulls eye and a proficient craftsman sets a nail precisely where he wants it, God is ordering and directing your steps.

—86—

I have seen all the works that are done under the sun;
and indeed, all is vanity and grasping for the wind.
—Ecclesiastes 1:14 (NKJV)

Okay, children," Miss Thomas directed, "single file now." She talked as much with her hands as she did her mouth, constantly nudging, coaxing, and pulling our wiggling second grade class back into line as we filed into the long, dimly lit hallways of Jason Lee Elementary School. Wandering or straggling students were hurriedly shepherded back into the straight-and-narrow. More quickly than you might imagine, the entire hallway filled with noisy children, turning left and right as they jostled one another, giggling, completely unaware and disconnected from the serious nature of our drill.

Suddenly, the voice of the principal boomed down the hallway. "Children, I want you to lie on the floor, face down with your side against the wall, head to toe to each other. Listen carefully now, I want you to place your left arm in front of your face, and place your forehead on your left arm. Okay, good. Now everyone, lie still please, we're almost finished. Now, place your right hand firmly behind your neck, like this."

Every child raised his or her eyes for a moment to see what the principal was doing. Then we waited, as sirens wailed eerily for what seemed like forever. Soon the teachers would have us all back on our feet, and we would return, single file, to our classrooms.

Back in 1962, I didn't realize we were living in an era of history now known as the "Cold War." I also didn't realize that we elementary school students were routinely going through bomb drills for a potential nuclear attack from the Soviet Union.

Jason Lee was only miles and minutes from the Manhattan Project -- the government site developed for producing weapons-grade plutonium. I guess this activity made the Soviets nervous, because our town of Richland, Washington, became a primary target. Hence.... the routine bomb drills in the schools.

As I reflect on this part of my life, I realize that the position we students assumed on that cold tile floor would have had absolutely no protective quality whatsoever.

From a nuclear blast, are you kidding me? As least, we were comfortable at ground zero. It was, at best, an exercise in futility or put another way "a useless action that cannot succeed."

Solomon offers us many other examples in his book of Ecclesiastes. King Solomon had a great deal to say about the futility of striving, clutching, grasping and driving for possessions, positions, and power. Pursuing too much work, wealth, or pleasure, according to Solomon, was like chasing the wind.

Chasing the wind? That's another great exercise in futility in Richland, Washington. There's plenty of it, but chase all you like, you'll never catch and hold it. To even try would be an impossible and utterly exhausting exercise, leaving one with a sense of the meaninglessness of life.

The core of Solomon's dilemma (and depression) in Ecclesiastes was his focus -- where he continually fixed his eyes. We all know that we tend to drive toward whatever we're looking at. (Just ask any woman who rides in the car with a man who can't keep his eyes on the road.)

Solomon used the phrase "under the sun" twenty nine times in Ecclesiastes. Perhaps his perspective would have been transformed had he focused "above the sun" -- to Creator God.

Fixated as he was on the "here and now," however, he become consumed with the "what ifs" and the "I don't haves" of life. Every new toy and new experience soon lost its luster "under the sun." As it always will.

—87—

What a God we have! And how fortunate we are to have
him.... Because Jesus was raised from the dead, we've been
given a brand-new life and have everything to live for,
including a future in heaven—and the future starts now!
—1 Peter:1-4 (MSG)

I have learned a great deal about the future by walking in the ruins of the past. Moving through the remnants of a Roman Cardo, staring at artifacts of a once strong and now vanished world reminds me that change is not an option... it is a simple fact of existence. My grandfather's world had disappeared. My dad's era is no more. Time and space march on and my own life experiences, even today, show me that the world I grew up in is now a vanished civilization -- a world that has come to an end in my lifetime.

As REM used to sing, "The world has come to an end and I feel fine." This is indeed a wonderful time to be alive. But in order to experience the full flow of life, you must put your face, not your back, to the future; you must look the future square in the eyes and see the horizon with the eyes of faith.

I once read a story about a man entering a country store. He made his way across the old porch to the entrance, where a vintage screen door hung silently on rusty hinges. He noticed the long spring, which would pull the door closed once he walked in. Inside, he stood still for a moment so his eyes could adjust to the dim light. Surveying the space, he saw relics from the past: an old cracker barrel, a large crock of dill pickles and one of those old time chest coolers, filled with ice water and cold Coca-Colas. He also saw a sign just in front of him and to the left of the door, which read: "Danger! Beware of dog!" The man quickly scanned the area until his eyes fell on a harmless old hound asleep near the counter.

"Is that the dog we're supposed to beware of?" he asked.

"Yep," said the old storekeeper.

"Well, he doesn't look dangerous to me," said the man. "Why the sign?"

The old man looked up through bushy eyebrows and said, "Because before I posted that sign, people kept tripping over him."

In many ways, our biggest dangers come not from getting bit by the future, but by not seeing the future clearly and then tripping over it.

I suggest that following Christ Jesus gives us peace in our past, joy in our present and hope for our future.

—88—

No eye has seen, no ear has heard, and no mind has imagined
what God has prepared for those who love Him. But it was to
us that God revealed these things by His Spirit. For His Spirit
searches out everything and shows us God's deep secrets.
—1 Corinthians 2:9-10 (NLT)

When I was about five years old, my dad worked as a heavy equipment operator, building hydroelectric dams along the Columbia River. We lived in a small town along the Columbia called Wishram, the site of ancient fishing villages and the point where the Columbia Gorge begins its cut west to the Pacific Ocean.

Whenever I could plan some kind of escape, I would take my two-year-old brother, Jack, by the hand and (to my mother's horror) attempt to teach him to climb the basalt bluff that hedged us in against the river. Jack and I would play around the house with Community Cat, conquering kingdoms and waging wars. Community Cat belonged to no one and yet everyone in Wishram, coming and going as he pleased and took his food and companionship wherever he could find it.

I specifically remember the cat, because of the time I had somehow managed to stuff it into one of my mom's empty five-pound coffee cans, sealed with a plastic lid. But then, when I wanted to release our furry friend, *I couldn't get the lid off.*

Jack and I made our way through the back porch screen door, then another door, leading directly into the kitchen

-- where Mom busied herself preparing dinner. "Mom," I said, "I can't get the lid off this can!" I held it up as high as I could reach, placing it into her hands.

I can't remember why I hadn't told her about Community Cat being in the can -- and at age four, I really don't think I had intended to pull a prank on her (or be cruel to our loyal animal pal, for that matter).

With Jack watching silently to one side, Mom carefully placed the can in the large, white, double sink and begin to pull the lid off. I can see the scene so clearly in my mind's eye. Mom was wearing a dress with an apron. As I stood by her side, looking up at her face, I could not see the can. But when the lid came off, I did see Community Cat shoot straight up into the air and my mom's face suddenly change shape as her mouth went into a silent scream -- just before she passed out on the kitchen floor. Jack and I stood there looking at her as the cat jumped off the counter making a bee-line through the screen door on the way to high ground. When Mom came to, I followed the cat as fast as I could.

Until Mom pulled the lid off the can, the contents remained hidden and unrevealed. Once the lid came off, boy, was she surprised! It was not what she expected.

Do you see the word "revealed" in 1 Corinthians 2:10? The Greek verb is *apokalypto*. It's a term that means to "uncover" or "disclose." This word is strategically positioned next to the Greek noun *apokalypsis*, which is translated "revelation," as in the last book of the Bible. Here's another way to say it: *apokalypto* means to take the lid off.

It is essential that we identify who has the power and privilege to *apokalypto* or take the lid off in order that we might *see, hear,* and *consider* what was previously hidden and unknown. Who has such a privilege? It is the Holy Spirit.

Dick Mills writes, "We can always relate to the past, because we have it in memory. We can always relate to the present, because of our five senses. The future is purposely concealed from us, and reminds us of how dependent upon the Lord we are for everything."

The Holy Spirit is our helper, guide, comforter, and teacher. He is the One who has the revelation for our future. He is the most high and ultimate "Knower" and "Seer." When times and seasons and cycles of life are easy, we need His insight in order to make wise decisions about our future (James 3:17-18). How much more must we follow His leadership in tough times! He protects us in "perilous times" so we thrive, not merely survive.

How do I know this is true? Well, going back to the Scripture with which I opened: "No eye has seen, no ear has heard, and no mind has imagined what God has prepared for those who love Him." (1 Corinthians 2:9) Since human vision, hearing and thinking cannot imagine that, don't be too shocked or surprised when He pulls the lid off.

—89—

When they heard the roaring in the sky above the house,
crowds came running to see what it was all about,
and were stunned to hear their own languages
being spoken by the disciples.
—Acts 2:6 (TLB)

Anyone who hangs out with me much at all soon learns that paths, trails and mountains are intersecting points of life where the Holy Spirit often speaks to me, teaches me and transforms my perspective. He changes my heart in wild places and sometimes high places.

My wife Nancy, daughter Hannah and her fiancé, Ben, along with son, Ethan, worked to construct a Native training center just off old Route 66 in Arizona. We were joined by Bill and Tammy Henshaw to help the Hualapai, (pronounced Walapai), who live along the western part of the Grand Canyon on one million acres. Together we poured concrete, moved earth, built awnings and helped finish the last tier of the roof.

About one hundred miles east is the south rim of the Grand Canyon. Have you seen it? What words are there to translate the color, vastness, beauty and terror? Ancient layers of geologic strata tell stories of the eons of time where incredible heat, raw physics and massive movement shaped this mile deep fracture where the Colorado River runs ice cold and race horse fast.

The last day we were in Arizona, we drove to the south rim and met George and Wendy Midbust. After last minute preparations, George, Bill and I, launched off Bright Angel Trail to traverse the rim-to-rim, finishing up the Kaibab trail on the north at eighty two hundred feet. As a raven flies, it is ten miles across. Our way was twenty-six miles with more than eleven thousand foot elevation change. We finished in 9.5 hours.

During the course of that day, I met people with a number of different responses to what we were doing. Some of them were bewildered, not understanding what moved us to do such a thing. Others were impressed, and some were inspired; but some of them laughed mockingly and said we were crazy. In fact, they were quite vocal in making fun of us. Nonetheless, we finished. It was not easy, though. With every step down into the canyon the temperature rose. Thousand foot rock walls sucked all the moisture out of my body. Thankfully our families had driven around the canyon to pick us up on the north rim, requiring almost as much time to make the drive as we required to run and hike the trails.

After returning home, I pondered all the responses people exhibit when you move outside the norm, reach out beyond the expected in dimensions and degrees, which they do not understand. *It reminded me of Pentecost.*

Pre-Pentecost, Jesus laid out the prophetic pattern for the Holy Spirit's energy, empowerment and equipping in and through the church in Acts 1:8.

Post Pentecost, standing on the dark abyss of the nations, one hundred twenty people were now ready in the grace of God's Spirit to step off the rim and into the unknown to take the good news to every dialect on earth.

Acts 2 outlines people's response: verse 6 says some were disturbed... verse 7 informs us that some admired them... verse12 states some responded with doubt... and verse 13 points out there were also some who jeered and made fun of them.

They kept running the race before them. Why? Because God caused their paths to cross for a purpose and down into the vastness of the nations they went facing the beauty and the terror before them. Moreover, they finished their call as each succeeding generation since then have done.

So will we. God has crossed our paths for a purpose.

Wow, look at that view.

—90—

*Don't you see that children are G*od*'s best gift?*
—Psalm 127:3 (MSG)

One of the first trail races I ran was the Moscow (Idaho) Mountain Madness trail run in September of 1994. The official website says, "The Moscow Mountain Madness Run began in 1978, with some sixty pioneering runners. You need to be in good shape to participate. This is the toughest of the Palouse Road Runner events. The course is mostly dirt logging road & single-track trails. It passes through beautiful timbered country, with occasional spectacular views over the Palouse."

As I recall, the course then was about twelve miles covering the spine of Moscow Mountain. In my mind, and according to the delirious state I was in, the first six miles were straight up and the last six miles were straight down. Of course, it was not this drastic but it felt that way.

What saved me from becoming a cynical, former, EX, and past trail runner was my youngest son, Ethan, who was just shy of his third birthday.

After what seemed like a week and half, I crossed the finish line and collapsed.

Ethan walked over to me and with scientific curiosity asked, "Dad, what are you doing?" I did not have a reasonable answer for him; so, I responded with, "I am just laying here." "What are you doing?" I asked him. He leaned over close to me, peered

237

into my blood shot eyes, which grimaced through waves of sweat and said, *"I have you some treasures!"*

He opened up his thick little fingers from both hands and revealed an assortment of odds and ends that made me smile; a tiny pine-cone, old rifle casing, a stick and a small stone. Suddenly, I was energized. Ethan made my heart dance in the middle of my mountain madness mindset. His small treasures were really medals of the most valuable kind. I got up, took him by the hand and said, "Let's go find something to eat!"

The Spirit and the bride say, "Come."
Let anyone who hears this say, "Come." Let
anyone who is thirsty come. Let anyone who
desires drink freely from the water of life.

Revelation 22:17 (NLT)

EPILOGUE

"Don't you see that children are <u>God's best gift</u>? The fruit of
the womb His generous legacy?" Psalm 127:3 (MSG)

What unspoken legacy do you hope to leave for your
children, grandchildren and great-grandchildren?
Like mist covering a mountain lake, that question hovers
over my mind, silently rising and falling, shifting, moving across the
edges of my mind it gently touches the surface of my heart.

The unusually gifted and prophetic band, "Mercy Me" sings
a song they call, In the Blink Of An Eye" which captures the
essence of this misty experience with the lyrics, "Time will fly,
but until then I embrace every moment I am given. There is a
reason I am living for a blink of eye."

Poignant words and they seep into the radius of my life. You
see, I realize that the radius of my life is directly connected to
how I connect to Christ and transmit that relationship to my
children. If the radius becomes more or shrinks into less is up to
me. Parents are transmitters and children are receivers. Would
you agree that the word "transmit" is apropos?

Our children watch us more than they listen to us and as they watch
how we do life, we transmit a life message to them.

I am hopeful that the blink of an eye we have been given will
transmit a life message to our children and beyond. A spoken
legacy that includes:

- Unabated Passion for Jesus and the Gospel.

- Contagious Child-like Faith in God to pull off the impossible.
- Untamed Adventurous spirit in fulfilling their God given purpose.
- Constant Synergy of living in real forgiveness; it's the Promised Land.
- Authentic love for one another, and others.
- Kingdom Vision, focus and persistence.
- Alertness to the rich value of family, a community of faith and Country.
- God's gift of friends and a few will last a life-time.

The mist is real.

Contact Information and Resources

Global Gateway Network
P.O. Box 1207
Richland, WA 99352

www.globalgatewaynetwork.org
globalgatewaynetwork@gmail.com

PERMISSIONS

ENDORSEMENTS FROM LEADERS

Micah Smith has traveled throughout the world, which has given him a special understanding of God's love through the eyes of the least, and the greatest.

Micah has long been heralded as a voice of God's wisdom. For those he loves, those he surrounds, and those he reaches out to- -all are blessed. In *Heaven's Heartbeat*, Micah uses practical ideas to illustrate biblical truths, while challenging readers to pursue the application of God's wisdom in their own lives. I highly recommend this book to the entire community of readers. The miracle of God's love is eloquently displayed in each devotion.

Michele McNeill
Author, *Finding a Friendship with God*

Micah Smith is a man of destiny. He carries a global vision in touching many nations. Included in this networking are his connections with Israel, with both civil and spiritual leaders. Incredibly, his ministry has also connected with the global Anabaptist nations, Amish, and Mennonites. These connections have in the past five years developed in a close relationship and joint missions with the Anabaptists on a vast scale.

It is without question, it was by divine design that my path crossed with Micah a number of years ago where our ministries converged, broadening both of our visions, together, with corporate ventures on the mission field.

Micah is a man who carries a clear focus on the Kingdom, he does not allow himself to be deterred by secondary issues,

Micah Smith

but marches forward, towards the goal of his high calling. This has ignited in me, a deeper passion for Gods kingdom purposes in my own life.

Bishop Ben Girod,
Founder of Anabaptist Connections Ministry,
www.anabaptistconnections.org

Wow, Micah's book is both encouraging and inspiring. Each new day I look forward to Micah's unique perspective on God's heartbeat sent to us from heaven. I encourage you to let his book bless your life on a daily basis, as it does mine.

Brad Klippert (Washington State Representative- 8ᵗʰ District)
Benton County Deputy
LTC Army National Guard

Micah Smith is a colleague of mine. Our work together began with leading a 35 member medical team to Global Gateway Network's new home for children in northern Vietnam. Shortly after, I became aware of Micah's gift of leading Christians to a deeper level of faith because he cares about the health and growth of the church globally. He has a great compassion to help others both physically and spiritually. He comes along side individuals in need and builds them up. He shares his writings in newsletters and briefs and has been encouraged by many believers to publish his writing. His work in Heaven's Heartbeat has the potential to be translated into many languages to build up believers who are being persecuted for Christ because Micah has experienced the persecution of Christians in India and other places. The experiences he has had in the Lord's work have enriched his writings. I highly recommend Heaven's Heartbeat because it is uplifting and demonstrates mercy, grace and compassion.

Lorna Schumann, PhD, NP-C, ACNS, BC,
ACNP, BC, CCRN, FAANP
Washington State University, College of Nursing,
Spokane, Washington

248

Micah Smith has the ability to use the ordinary to illustrate the extraordinary hand of God. With heartfelt words, he tells true stories from everyday living that refreshes, inspire, and teach—all pointing to the power of faith.

Lucy Luginbill, *Tri-City Herald*
Spiritual Life editor and blogger
(www.tri-cityherald.com/lightnotes) Kennewick, Washington

I have known Micah Smith since 2000 when he became my pastor at Richland Assembly of God Church in Richland, Washington. I served on the elder board with him for several years and found him to be a man of great integrity and totally sold out to God. More than any other pastor I have had, he had and still has, a burning passion to reach the lost especially unreached people groups.

As I spent time with Micah I found that this passion began to infect me and as a result, I took my first overseas mission trip with him to Southeast Asia in 2001. Twelve years later, I found myself first in Thailand and now Cambodia as a missionary, in part, because of his leadership and his heart to reach the lost.

Now I consider Micah Smith to be not only a mentor, but also a friend that I can go to for spiritual direction as well as for wisdom and support. During the time, he was my pastor, I found that his words both spoken and written conveyed a deep understanding of God that was expressed in easily understood terms. I particularly found his ability to see God at work in nature where Micah has spent so much of his time and in every day events that most people do not see. I believe that readers of this book will find themselves enriched and inspired in their walk with our Lord Jesus Christ.

Eugene F. Pratt
Retired Judge, Benton County district court & Itinerant
Missionary

It was at a family reunion in Oklahoma some years ago where I first met Micah Smith, he being a true blooded second cousin. As it has been with very few people in my life, whom I could count on one hand, upon my meeting Micah, a genuine Holy Spirit connection was made! Even though distance has kept us physically separated much of the time that spiritual connection has remained intact through the years.

Immediately after my initial meeting up with him, I learned through both physical and spiritual observation, that the name of Micah Smith was synonymous with "adventure" – spiritual adventure! His adventuresome spirit, which I believe wholeheartedly to have been wrought and placed within him by God himself, continues to intrigue and amaze me today.

Micah has indeed responded to the divine call of great adventure in the Kingdom of God and his travels into foreign and remote lands in effort to spread God's Word, reach "unreached" people groups, plant churches, build orphanages, and otherwise distribute humanitarian aid to those far less fortunate than we – is beyond remarkable! Being quite the "wordsmith", Micah has with unique ability, here within, drawn the spiritual out of the natural and displayed in personal account the coupling of faith and works, in his extraordinary adventures with God.

Jon Smith, Pastor – Rock Harbor Church, Ravia, OK
Sheriff – Johnston County, OK

About the Author

Micah is the founder and president of Global Gateway Network, a nonprofit organization helping complete the Great Commission of Christ. Since 2002 he has worked with professional volunteers in leading medical teams, developing clean water systems and building homes for children. Micah is an avid trail runner and roasts coffee. He and his wife Nancy, have five children and live in Moyie Springs, Idaho. Visit him online at www. globalgatewaynetwork.org